"Over hills and mountains and to Amerikay . . ."

Ramblin' With Micho Russell:
Ireland's Legendary Tin Whistler and Beloved Folk-musician

By

Dennis C. Winter

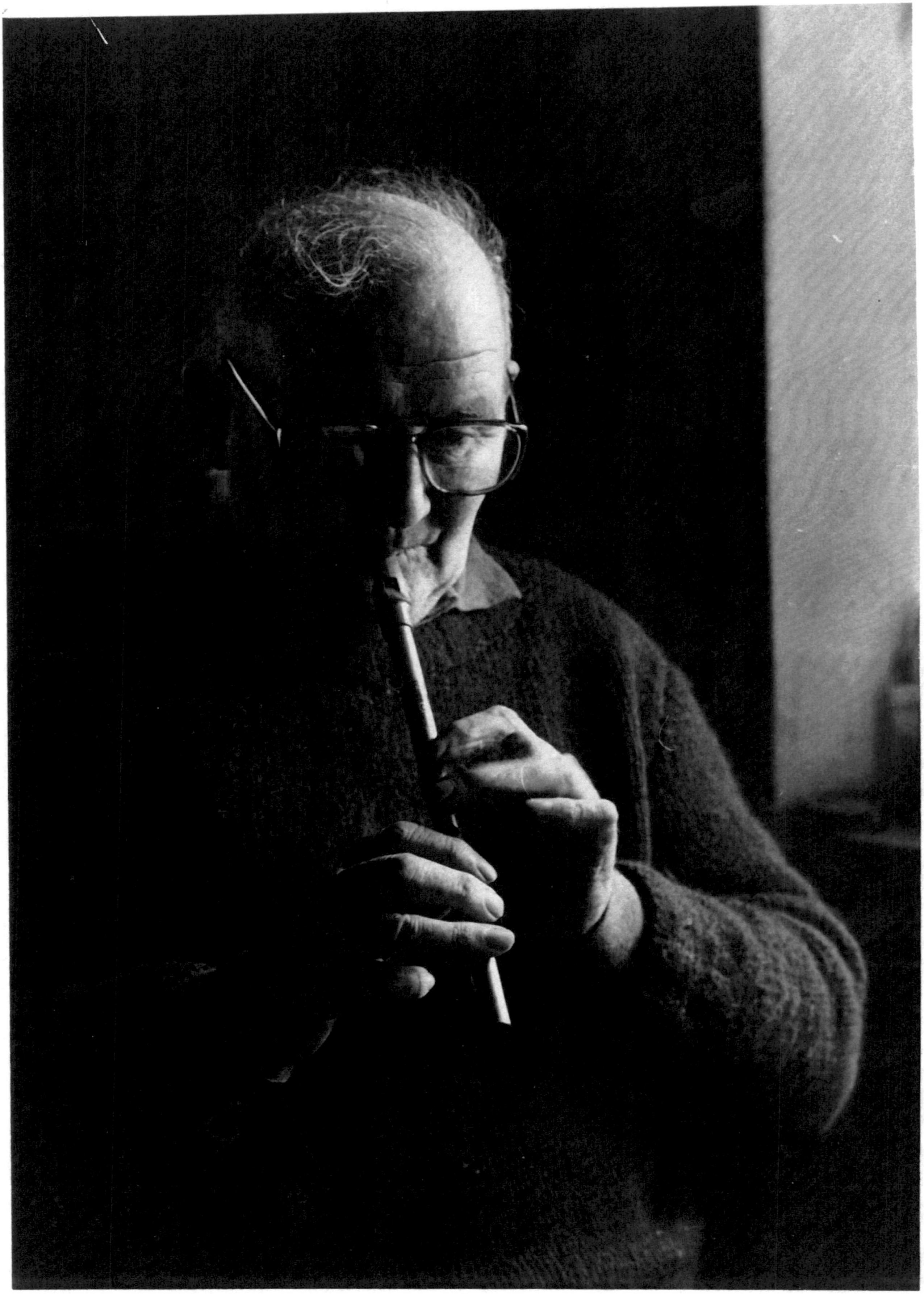

Dedicated To:

Stephen, Luke, and Travis;

Good kids, fine men.

And

In Memoriam:

Michael Boyne Dunleavy

1994 – 2002 (R.I.P.)

First published by
Dennis C. Winter
July 7, 2011

Printing of First Limited Edition
provided by:
Canal Press, Rosendale, NY
and
Finelli Pizza, Ellsworth, ME

Copyright © 2014 by Dennis C. Winter

All rights reserved. This book or any portion thereof may not be reproduced or used in any manner whatsoeverwithout the express written permission of the publisherexcept for the use of brief quotations in a book review.

All photographs © Dennis C. Winter unless otherwise noted.

Printed in the United States of America

First Printing, 2011
Second Printing, 2014

D.C. Winter
276 Second Avenue
Kingston, NY 12401
(845) 594-2527

winterd@earthlink.net
www.denniscwinter.com

ISBN 978-0-578-14550-1
LCCN 2014911631

Preface - A Memoir for all Seasons

Gearóid Ó hAllmhuráin

Long before cellphones and high-speed internet shrunk the world into the palm of one's hand, people living in rural communities were often keenly aware of the topographical and cultural differences that set them apart from metropolitan 'centres' of civilization. The remote rural *clachán* of Fisherstreet, or Doolin, on the windswept coast of Clare was one such place. Cut off behind the Cliffs of Moher that tower above the fury of the Atlantic, Doolin was at once on the edge of the old world and on the edge of the new - looking west to America, its neighboring parish.

When Ireland's legendary tin whistle player, Micho Russell, was born in Doonagore above the village of Doolin in 1915, the world was drowning in a tide of mass slaughter: the Great War that would end all wars was in full flight determined to impose a new world order at any cost. The history of mankind would change irrevocably in its wake. Closer to home, Irish rebels plotted political insurrection, while the merchants of Ennis, Limerick, and Galway presided over economic life in the relatively stable midwest of Ireland that was ravaged by the Great Famine a generation before. In the small farms and seasonal fishing grounds of Doolin, time and space unfurled on a very different scale. This was a milieu where walking distances governed the daily lives of people. A journey to Ennistymon, the nearest market town five miles to the south, was a major undertaking on foot, or with a horse and cart. Work in this coastal place followed the rounds of the seasons: tillage in spring, hay in summer, harvest in autumn, repairs to tools, nets, and inside chores in winter. Long before radio and television dominated family life and cars ferried people beyond the prying eyes of neighbors to diversions far away, 'passing the time' was regulated by the ritual of the *cuaird* and the *ragairne* with their intimate gatherings of storytellers, musicians, and dancers. It was in this archaic world that Micho Russell honed his music, song, and dance along with his brothers, friends, and neighbors for the first sixty years of his life.

When American ethnographer, Dennis Winter, rambled into O'Connor's pub in Doolin in 1981, the world on the edge of the old world was a very different place. Two more world wars had come and gone, global order had been broken and restored several times, and Ireland was no longer shackled to the throne of a monarch. Doolin now was awash with cars and tourists, few of whom cared about the neighbors, nor the walking distances that marked the boundaries of an older time. The countercultural *zeitgeist* spawned by the anti-war, civil rights and women's movements had finally coalesced with the transatlantic hippy scene and had found its way into the most unlikely parts of rural Ireland, not least Doolin, which was thronged with young Americans seeking respite from the small wars and sprawling suburban jungles of Uncle Sam. In the three small public houses that dot the two-mile streetscape of *Sráid na nIascairí*, these young Yanks mingled with locals and students from the university towns of Europe exploring the cultural byways of their recently extended European Economic Community. Doolin, on the western edge of the Burren, had become an Irish music mecca, an *entrepôt* of cultural tourism that surprised even Irish tourist planners at the time. The linch pin of this global tide was Micho Russell who was 'discovered' in the early 1970s, after half a century eking a sparse living on a hungry coastal farm. Emerging from a lifestyle that was the very antithesis of modernity, his odyssey into the staged world of professional music was rare and incongruous. Dennis Winter was a witness to this remarkable process.

Winter was not just another 'vas in Doolin' visitor. This moniker, with its wily hint of *searbhús* in a village overwhelmed by long-haired strangers, was reserved for less discerning travelers who passed through fleetingly before moving on to find themselves in another corner of the cosmos. A seasoned cultural traveller, Winter came to Doolin with a writer's ear for a good story, a personal quest for good music, and a past career in submarine warfare that he kept very much to himself. Ironically, this quiet personal saga found an echo in the life and times of another submarine warrior, John Philip Holland, 'The Man who Invented the Submarine,' who was born in nearby Liscannor in 1840. Winter got to know the inner world of Fisherstreet by making friends with local characters, quietly observing their folkways, and sitting in discreetly on the edge of their sessions. Over time, his lively coterie included raconteur, Brud Petty, *seanchaí* Paddy Shannon, last of the native Irish speakers in Clare, the eccentric Killoughery brothers, John and Paddy, and the celebrated Russells, Gussie and Micho: the former, a bashful 'shy class of a man,' his brother Micho, a simple yet complex man whose travels had taken him into the far corners of Europe. In this moving memoir, Dennis Winter speaks to us about two transatlantic journeys and two transatlantic travelers: himself and Micho, each, in his own way, discovering the other's place in the universe.

Over Hills and Mountains and to Amerikay does exactly what it sets out to do. It enthralls the reader with a remarkable musical travelogue, beginning with the cultural topography of the West of Ireland before crossing the Atlantic to the concrete corridors of New York, Boston, and Philadelphia, and finally coming to rest in the pristine wilderness of the Hudson Valley. Here in this primal forest, where Rip Van Winkle slept so soundly, Micho discovered the world of Washington Irving and the hospitality of Pete Seeger, folk icon and guardian of New York's great river. Along the way, we are regaled with tales of discovery, ethnographic anecdote, hilarious observation, and moments of intense spiritual reflection, as narrator and musician engage with each new encounter through their own personal languages and philosophies. Underpinning all these peregrinations is an enduring sense of wonder and respect for Micho Russell, and an empathy for his older world where the tune was indeed 'brother to the prayer.' *Treise leat, A Dhennisín* for bringing us along on such a timeless adventure. Through your words and images, the old man with the cap from Doolin with a whistle in his pocket and a prayer in his heart will indeed 'keep on goin'' and, along the way, make new friends in the most unlikely places.

Professor Gearóid Ó hAllmhuráin, MA, DUEF, MBA, Ph.D.
Johnson Chair in Quebec and Canadian Irish Studies
School of Canadian Irish Studies
Concordia University Montreal
August 15, 2011

"We must remember the living man." – Michael Coady

My first meeting with Michael "Micho" Russell, Ireland's renowned and celebrated tin whistler and folk musician, took place "way below in Doolin" (as the song goes), his home village, way out on the edge of the Atlantic near the mouth of Galway Bay in northwest Co. Clare. It was a magical confrontation that has been a formative influence on my life ever since. I write about that chance meeting on one cold and windy, but truly magical winter weekend in the early 1980s, my very first visit to Ireland, in much further detail in, *Those Days in Doolin: My Times with the Tradition-makers*. To set the stage for this memoir at hand, though, which is specifically based on my later travels with the late, great Micho Russell, I offer this short excerpt from that larger work of ethno-biographical, folkloric memoir:

> Upon introducing myself to Micho and spending that first Saturday evening in Ireland with him at Gus O'Connor's Pub, as the night wound to a close and the last call: "Now lads, please . . ." was sounded, Micho asked: "Have you the car?" I replied I did indeed. "There's a bit of a dance we could ramble off to," he added. And off we drove to an after-hours dance being held in the Claremont Hotel over in the seaside resort village of Lahinch. These dances were held as benefits for some sports team or charitable group, or other, and one of the added benefits of these events was that they extended legal drinking hours well into the morning -- Pubs were closing at 11:00 pm, for the most part, back then.
>
> Along with our tickets for entrance, we also received a cooked chicken dinner back then, which was greatly relished by Micho, always fond of a good feed, and particularly so that night by myself, since I hadn't eaten much that day save for a toasted sandwich. As we ate our late-night dinner, we sat and enjoyed watching the dancers; a mixed crowd of young and old, waltzing and dancing polkas to a *Céilí* band, with a few traditional "sets" mixed in. Later along, the theme of the dance tended to lean towards disco, with mostly young folks out on the floor under the disco-lights. I could sense Micho's enjoyment as he watched the youthful dancers. I wasn't sure then, as I was only just getting to know him, but I sensed he was an older man with an artistic nature, one who could realize and appreciate what true classical beauty was, not unlike great artists of the stature of a Pablo Picasso or his friend and contemporary, Georges Braque -- both remained true appreciators of classical beauty into their late years, no matter how modern their works had become during the progression of their careers.
>
> As we watched examples of this natural phenomenon in the form of young, beautiful Irish girls dancing under the disco lights, I asked what he thought of this rock-and-roll and disco-dancing?, and I will never forget his reply: " Ah, Faith, to tell you the truth I don't see much charity in it." I knew then I was in the company of a thoughtful, gentle and caring man. As I came to know him closely over the next decade, I did come to the realization that he was like many of his generation who had missed out on the

chances for youthful marriages and were now entering their 60s; still they held out great hope and longed deeply for a wife. And why wouldn't he? Why wouldn't any of these members of what Brud Petty, one of Micho's Doolin contemporaries (famed for his recitations), so aptly called the "lonely generation" – the ones who stayed home on the land; why wouldn't they wish for a bride? Having been handsome, attractive, land-owning young men, why wouldn't they, though seemingly late in life, wish for that same elusive and natural state-of-being called marriage that so many of these lads, the last of the post-famine bachelors, craved and never knew? The wish to enjoy the compansion-hip of a loving spouse lived on in many of these older bachelor-farmers, and sadly, many men of their generation in the region simply missed out on that part of life; and for many more reasons than can be discussed here.

That Saturday night in Lahinch, though, by the time the dance and event finally had come to a close, I realized this had become a really long second- day in Ireland for me, and in the early morning hours of Sunday, we headed home to Doolin. We rolled on up over the hill, taking the shortcut in a northwesterly direction, up along a back road from Liscannor; past the old quarry sites up in Doonagore where the tall radio "mast" (antennae, to me) stood. As the bright winter moon illuminated the landscape, the gorgeous, clear-winter-night's view of Galway Bay and the Aran Islands stretched out before our eyes. This was his neighborhood, I thought, as Micho took his whistle out from "the inside pocket of his outside coat" and began to play a distinct, clear as a bell, tune on his whistle for me. A priceless moment -- it was a march: "Gary Owen," a tune I had heard in the States, usually associated with the American Civil War.

He asked me: "Have you ever heard of this man called General Custer?" I said I had, and he continued: "Well, the pipers in his army were playing this tune, and there was a man called, Sitting Bull. This man, Sitting Bull, didn't like this tune at all, and he had his braves and warriors scalp 'em all!" Wow, I thought. I never knew! But I did resolve at that moment to write about this incredible man, musician, and unaffected storyteller. And to be sure, he was a wonder. And here he was smiling and sitting next to me in that little blue, Fiat hire-car, basked in the moonlight above Galway Bay, like some kind of Celtic Musical Buda-like Minstrel-cum-Druidic Bard; something definitely out of the pure realm of folklore that I recognized immediately. I don't think I'd ever felt luckier than I did that night. To this day I'm not quite sure why I felt so elated. But I guess I could never have dreamed of, or made up such a pure moment of rare, human experience; nor could I ever have imagined at that time, the amazing experiences that would follow as we rambled together in the years to come.

At the outset of this particular memoir, I do not want to infer that other rare musical and magic-seeming figures like Micho didn't exist to be met at that time, or are now so nearly extinct that they are beyond the reach of those seeking original experiences in the realm of Irish folk culture. I do feel quite safe in saying at the beginning of this discussion and story of my rambles with him, however, that almost anyone who ever met Micho, (pronounced Mike-O), at anytime or at any place while he was with us here on earth, undoubtedly has their own special tale to tell about him and that meeting, I would also venture to say that it was an experience wherein they felt they were in the presence of someone special; charming, larger than life, and of whom many, many people have voiced the old saws concerning the one-of-a-kind nature of his being, which is epitomized by the "broken mold" metaphor, and it's true, too; there was only the one-and-only Micho Russell.

Micho's unique personality and music were of such a blend that one couldn't always discern where one left off and the other began, but without doubt, the likes of his particular, total persona will certainly rarely be seen or heard again for many, many moons. His tin whistle and flute playing, and his singing remains for us on recordings as testaments to his originality of sound, style and phrasing, and there are also a good few videos available that still afford us a glimpse of the living man. While it's an understatement to say he was a born rambler and loved to travel, which was something we both had in common, he also had a life-long, deep and abiding love for his own autochthonic, deeply rooted sense of place in a rural farming parish on the Western Seaboard of Ireland where he was born, raised and lived his entire life on the same farm of land. He also possessed a deep, lifelong love of the music of that place; this being another thing we had in common from the start, the music within our reach: regional, traditional folk music. It is also safe to say that he represented, for many, a fading, sentimental (perhaps) last glimpse of traditional, rural Irish ways, and by that I mean not just old-fashioned tunes and playing styles; but also ways of being, ways of getting along in life, ways of speaking and using language, and how he put his own personal stamp on expressing this journey through life via his music and voice. He was folklore walking, as far as I'm concerned – a rare one when he was among us, for sure.

Micho's grand, soft, Clare accent alone, could fairly well melt you. I recall early on, as I began driving him around Ireland on what became yearly excursions for me, hearing him say something as simple as: "The poor ould cat . . ," as we passed an unfortunate feline lying by the side of the road, who had met its life's fatal end on the highway. I tell can tell you, it would just melt your heart to hear it. I also never saw him miss a genuflection as we passed church, graveyard, or priest; you name it, if he thought it was Holy he made the sign of the cross. In all, it is safe to say he was a gentle and pious fellow. And, although he seemed to have more than one foot steeped in the distant Irish past, he still managed to travel throughout the modern world and all around his beloved native Ireland, and to many foreign places as well; mostly by having been invited to come there as a professional musician and to perform for hundreds and even thousands, sharing whole-heartedly as he went along his wondrous and charming music. But without his abiding faith and good heart, I doubt he would have got the pluck to travel out so far. Many of his contemporary, bachelor-farmer friends and local "musicianers," as he called them, in Doolin Parish, rarely travelled out of the County Clare, let alone to Germany, Norway, Brittany, England and not last nor least, across the wide Atlantic "and to Amerikay."

I may have suggested to Micho that he come visit me in America as we parted ways on one of my early visits to Doolin spent traveling and playing music with him, and that idea may have been fairly lighthearted at the time. But, as I said my farewells before heading back to my home in the States, we shared the sense that that may indeed be an adventure which could actually happen. At that early date, it was probably also a way of saying that I, too, think you are a special person, Micho, and I hope we meet again soon and maybe you will come visit us in the Hudson River Valley, in upstate New York. I definitely had said I would try to write about him in the near future at the very least, and that I would be back again to go rambling around Ireland and play music with him and meet all numbers and types of people, and go collecting songs and tunes and stories. These ambitions we also had in common and we seemed to hit it off as musicians sometimes do.

There was something else between Micho and me that I suspect may most easily be categorized by an uncle/nephew, or father/son type of relationship that developed fairly quickly, as over the next few years I returned to Doolin and visited Micho, and we drove around Ireland together. My father, Bill Winter, had passed on several years before I ever got the notion to travel to Ireland, but he was of roughly the same generation as Micho, and his mother was an Irish-born woman; and as Micho and his brothers, Gussie and Packie, were all bachelors, there were sadly no sons to whom they could pass on their knowledge and their music to. This was a pity, but it is also a fact of their almost mythological history. That said, I was aware from the beginning that I was at the very least an apprentice, and that Micho was a willing teacher of music, tin whistle playing, and the ins and outs of the professional world of folk-music, and more importantly, perhaps, the art of enjoying life and the times we're in as we just "keep going."

As the 1980's rolled by, I managed to publish an essay or two on Micho and about Doolin, and re-published for MIcho a small folk-lore collection called: The Piper's Chair No. 2 in 1986. In that second edition (now in its fourth printing), I included some new photos and an essay entitled: "The Whistling Ambassador." It was my first attempt at trying to discuss and describe Micho, and it is just as difficult today as it was then to impart what it was like to be with him. Still, I press on . . . .

In 1990 I published a small monograph entitled: Doolin's Micho Russell:a Portrait, and with this and the previous mentioned book in hand, Micho and I delved further into the professional realm of his career at the time. His travelling and playing had been curtailed a bit during those years as he had been experiencing some physical ailments, particularly with a dry tear duct condition which hampered his activities considerably in those intervening years and also caused him considerable discomfort. His eye soreness and the need for eye-drops became a daily concern for "us," as we rambled off around the country. Often I recall hearing: "We forgot the eye drops." "Oh did we?" was my usual reply – it seemed there was always a bit of whimsy in the air around Micho.

One day we planned a trip into the city of Ennis, and I left Micho off at the laundry there to have some of his clothes cleaned, and he also had some other errands in town, and I agreed to meet him for tea at Brogan's back room by the bar after I did my own bits and pieces in town. After meeting him and enjoying a cup of tea and a sandwich, which he stood me, we headed back along the winding roads to Doolin and to his house, and I can see him now, standing and leaning-in beside the car as we watched the evening sun diminish over the Aran Islands to the west, and he saying: "Faith, We forgot the laundry!" "Oh, did we?" I said. "Perhaps we'll take a drive there tomorrow?" he asked. "Sure thing, Micho," God love the man, I thought. "Sure I'll collect you", I said. "Not too early," he reminded me. And more often than not, that next day's ramble would be full of fun and folklore and all sorts of unimaginable capers.

On another day we headed off to find a concertina for one of Micho's young students. Micho had great time for teaching youngsters and did so all through the years I knew him. Well, we wasted a good couple hours in a pub in Ennistymon that morning, listening to the bar owner tell of the wondrous concertina he owned, but in the finish-up, after Micho enquired would he be interested in selling it?, the man had said that he, "wouldn't sell it to St. Peter himself." Fair play to the barman, he'd told a good and entertaining yarn. We left undaunted, but I felt we'd been put-on, and that man probably had no concertina in his possession at all. But we took things like this in stride and headed off to a house outside of town where the answer we got from the woman of the house was, "Oh, I'm sorry to say, but Uncle Paddy had a concertina, but was buried with it some years ago." 'Twas a pity, we agreed.

At the next farmyard we stopped into late that afternoon, an aged and somewhat slightly wizened looking woman peered out from the open door of her cottage, and again said there was no concertina there, but she squinted and asked: "Is that you, Micho Russell?" Well, long story-short, she turned out to be Mary Ellen Reidy, a fiddler of some renown in her youth, and a player that Micho had played music with back in the 1940's. In we go for tea and cakes, and out I go to the car to get my fiddle for her to play on, and she and Micho had a great session that day playing the few tunes she could still manage; talking of old times, dances, and radio programs they had appeared on together in years gone by, and I was thrilled to be part of it and able to tape some of the music they made that day.

Needless to say, we never found a concertina that day, but we had had another great day on the road together, and as always we most likely ended up at O'Connor's Pub on Fisher Street that night to see who was there and usually to play some tunes, even on the most barren and quiet of winter nights.

I always found it a delight to hear Micho play his own unique batch of tunes, and the same goes for Gussie, his brother. Hearing them at their most relaxed and most comfortable moments at home or in O'Connor's on the quiet, have been unquestionably some of the finest musical experiences I've known. Gussie once played "The Leaving of Liverpool" for me on his timber-flute, in the car on the way back up to Doonagore, on a cold, wet, windy night after closing time, as a farewell gift to me before my leaving the next day – truly a beautiful moment.

There were many great sessions of music during those years that I recall fondly, many with both Micho and Gussie playing, but also many with my dear friend, Cyril O'Donoghue, whose ballad and folk singing and his impeccable bouzouki and guitar playing had caused me to regain and retain faith in the folk music world, and, in his words, to "keep the dream alive." Cyril had an instinctive ability to attract great melodic players those days like the fiddlers: Tola Custy, big Mick Queally, and the young Yvonne Casey, and the accordion and concertina player, Josephine Marsh. He was always kind to Micho and Gussie and the older lads like Paddy and John Killhoury who came in to play in those years. Cyril, like Eoin O'Neil and Tola and Mary Custy, always had enormous time for Micho and those older lads who we all related to as the true, local tradition-bearers. I also recall playing many fine sessions those years with Noel O'Donoghue (different family) the flute player; Terry Bingham, concertina; Kevin Griffin, banjo; Michel Bonamy, a flute-playing Breton wizard; Eugene Lambe the piper, his son, Ian Lambe, the guitarist, and eventually "Banjo Michelle" came to town from France, and Christie Barry came home from America. Seamus Creagh was the fiddler in town, up from Cork City for that weekend when I first ventured into O'Connor's in Doolin. He was an inspirational force to see and hear, and in those days any and everyone who truly loved playing the music made their way to town, including the likes of the Clancys, the Fureys, Jackie Daly and way too many more to mention here.

One memorable excursion Micho and I made one winter was way out to Clifden to see Brendan Flynn, the Headmaster of the Community School out there in the wilds of far western Connemara, the closet European land to America, where Alcock and Brown landed their first intercontinental flight, and also where Marconi's cable surfaced in Europe. Brendan was not only a devoted teacher and a Yeats scholar, but greatly appreciated the folk music traditions in Ireland. He was instrumental in explaining to me, early on, how rare Micho was, and in pointing out how very often in Ireland men like Micho were taken for granted in their home-towns and villages. Brendan had also founded the Clifden Community Arts Festival which is still going strong and has become one of the premier Arts Weeks in Ireland. He always had great time for Micho, and often included Micho in many programs out there; also having him (and myself, too, in later years) play for the students at the school, or included us on the Arts Week program. Micho always used the term "young scholars," when speaking of young school-children, and he absolutely revered teachers. He felt that to be a teacher was next only to the priesthood in importance and stature. Micho was very fond of Brendan Flynn, and thought extremely highly of him. Brendan's a man who can throw some light on a thing, as the saying goes, and a man who has devoted his life to teaching in his community and to exposing his community to the best of art, music, literature and folk culture, by bringing the great practitioners of those arts to Clifden.

We started out fairly early on that trip (for musicians anyway), on a fine sunny morning, and after a jaunting short-cut (down in North Carolina they say "near-cut") up the green road near Ballyvaughan, and a brief stop in Galway for lunch and a stop at the shoemaker's shop, on we drove. The weather turned against us a bit as we left Galway, and I flogged on at the wheel through a long, misty, rainy day, driving out through the bog-lands west of Galway with the mountains, the Twelve Pins, to our north; finally arriving way out in Clifden, only to find that Brendan had gone in to Galway for the day! "A bit of a disappointment," was Micho's summation, and off we went back eastward towards the interior of Connemara to try and barge our way into the Irish Language Radio station, Raidió na Gaeltachta, out somewhere near Ros a' Mhíl.

Micho was naturally thinking they would certainly welcome us with open arms and microphones and put us on-air immediately, etc. which, of course, did not happen. However, as we lost the last of the daylight hours, we stopped into a pub out there for a bit of grub. There we found a young barman in a fairly empty country pub, who, it turned out, could not only duplicate a couple tape cassettes for us on his dual-cassette boom-box, but also, after warming to us over some chat, offered that he also knew where we could get some *poteen* (Irish White-lightning), which Micho and Gussie both used and treasured, primarily as a lineament for their sore feet and achy bones. I also bought a large vodka-bottle-full, just for kicks and to bring back to a connoisseur publican friend of mine in the Catskills who owned a place called the Krumville Kountry Inn.

We made our purchase from an Irish-speaking farmer, out at a clandestine barn somewhere in the darkness of a Connemara farmyard, and our young guide, when I asked about getting back through customs in New York, said: "Sure you'll tell them it's Holy Water." That lad had said it with a great Connemara accent too, and I should add that Micho eventually came to the realization that he knew this young lad's father or uncle from the past, who was known to have been a fine dancer. Micho recalled having seen him do some "double battering" on top of a wooden crate placed out on the dance-floor, somewhere in the long ago.

Micho seemed to know people from far and wide and from long ago, including some who had been forgotten by their own relatives. Micho was also extremely keen at remembering names and faces. I remember that young barman lamenting to us that day how he felt the Irish Language that he and his siblings had grown up with would soon be lost, as once they grew up, he said; the trend was to drop it and stop using it. I think this trend may be reversing a bit today, but at the time, speaking Irish was in decline. Micho was always proud of the Irish language he did have, and the pieces in his performances that he recited or sang in Irish fondly express this. Regardless, he was in fine fettle that evening, even with our disappointment at not having met Brendan Flynn in Clifden, as we completed our round trip and landed back in to O'Connor's just before closing. It had been another long day's journey into the realm of folklore and myth with my good travelin' buddy, Micho Russell.

Another similar journey was to a wee village called Corr na Móna, north of Oughterard, way up on the north shore of Lough Corrib, to play a session up there at a pub owned by an American man, Bob Cohan, who also owned a pub in Saratoga NY, called The Parting Glass. We had a lovely afternoon of music with the local players up there. I remember Micho being rather taken with an accordion player who had come out for the afternoon, a middle-aged man with his family in tow, and with whom we had a great chat after the session had ended; even carrying on out into the parking lot before we left. I remember Micho distinctly saying to me later in the car that, "That was a true-born Irishman." Micho's take on people was usually spot-on -- highly perceptive, sensitive and insightful. Especially, one might think, coming from a countryman-farmer, but again, I think his nature was based in that sensitive world of the artist: quite the difficult balancing act I'm sure.

For instance, on our drive home that same evening we kind of begged our way into a tea shop in Cong (where the "Quiet Man" was filmed) just as the woman who ran it was about to close up for the day. We managed to purchase and wolf down a few sandwiches and tea, which were greatly appreciated by our famished wandering stomachs, and back in the car Micho pronounced: "Well, at least she didn't meet us with a domineering manner . . ." And once, after I had sung the praises of a fellow musician to Micho, someone who was also a musician as well as a skilled craftsman and successful businessman, and I'd said how impressed I was with the fellow, he responded: "But, . . . you know, he's a very unsettled man." Enough said . . . , I thought.

Around that time (late 1980's), I also fondly remember one night when we heard that Loreena McKennitt, the great Canadian singer and also a very beautiful woman, was in Clare and would be down to O'Connor's on a specific evening, and word had been sent to Micho to come down to appear for the occaision. Naturally, being his willing driver, I was going along too. I pulled up to his house early that evening to pick up him and Gussie for the lift down to Fisher Street. This I would have been doing anyway, but Micho explained again for me the special visit that was on for the night, and I must have looked a little haggard, because he also added: "You might want to have a bit of a shave. It can't hurt to put in your application, you know?"

One of the longest, and most memorable, and definitely one of the more important journeys we made together in Ireland was up to Dublin to tape the "Pure Drop" television show for RTE. It was produced by another Micho enthusiast and friend, the great accordionist, Tony McMahon. This show was an immaculate performance by Micho, and I believe a highlight for him at that time. It was also a hilarious drive through the country, to and fro, as was spending a couple days and nights in Blackrock, outside of Dublin, at the RTE studios for the taping. We were looked after first-rate, too -- put up nicely at a nearby B&B, and were paid nice stipends and travel vouchers as well. Eamon McGivney, the fiddler, had also joined up with us and was also on the program as well. He and I both found it quite handy that the RTE studio conveniently had a tremendous lounge-bar attached to the sound-stage area, and we agreed that RTE should get high marks for being such a first-class operation, for, as Eamon put it, a bit of lubrication for a fiddler is often needed because: "That fiddle can rear-up on you, you know?"

I remember meeting Tony McMahon for the first time at the studio, and being introduced to his assistant, Séan Potts, tin whistler in the Chieftains in the early days; and also to the director and staff. I also met the young "presenter" (host), Iarla Ó'Lionáird, and gave him my wee books, as he was somewhat unfamiliar with Micho, and I was thrilled when he actually quoted from the book during his on-air introduction, especially the quote from Bryan McMahon, the revered author from Listowel, Co. Kerry, referring to Micho as "one of the great men of Ireland."

Mr. Potts introduced me to the immaculately dressed Wardrobe Overseer, as: "Dennis Winter, MIcho's, ah . . . publisher." Somewhat mortified, I quickly replied that I was actually Mr. Russell's *chauffer,* and prepared to drive him anywhere. Micho then handed over to the Wardrobe Man a fairly rough looking and not all that white of a white shirt from his small travel bag (whistles, razor, eye-drops, not much else in there). The brilliant Wardrobe fellow, without missing a beat, said: "Sure, Micho, that'll be grand. We'll send it out for a wee pressing." And Micho looked smashing that evening for the live performance and taping. Just before he went on-camera, I gave his eye-glasses a quick cleaning and chuckled to myself as I remembered having asked Micho how well had Tony taken care of him out on tours in Germany and the like? And he had said: "He sometimes drives me distracted with making me clean the eye-glasses." Truth be told, Tony McMahon took great care of us in Dublin, and I know he thought the world of Micho.

The taping of the "Pure Drop" show went off beautifully, and I also recall that day was the day I learned Micho's version of the tune, "The Flannel Jacket," as he and the young players backing him up had rehearsed it many times that afternoon. Micho met his marks and timing perfectly that evening like a true professional. As I watched from a table on-set, along with another young man who had come down from Northern Ireland, and who was also due to play flute on the second show being taped that weekend, I was quite touched as he leaned over and whispered in a great Northern accent: "Is that your father?"

When the time came for us to leave Dublin, I recall getting a bit grumpy with Micho, as I foolishly expected him to know how we should head out of the inner city! I had ended up getting us stuck in brutal traffic, but after I studied the map a bit and found our way, and once we had rolled out towards the West, I relaxed, and we soon got a brain-wave to head south and go visiting down in Carrick-on-Suir, in Tipperrary. This is the home of his dear friends, Michael Coady, the poet and author, and Seamus McGrath, carpenter, folksinger and songwriter, and their respective families, and also Tom "the Bard" Power, who also lived down there on O'Mahony Ave. with his great big family, too. All were great fans and friends of Doolin and of the Russells.

We had a long drive and a brief, but warm visit at Michael Coady's house; heard a few tunes from Micho, and posed for a photo in the yard, which ended up In Michael's wonderful memoir: *The Well of Spring Water*. Then we finally headed north towards Clare, and back on homeward to Doolin, still a good long journey. I should add that all these travels were lengthened in time even more so by the natural necessity of an older man's need to have a leak, and especially so, when after whatever pub we stopped in to use the jacks, we usually had a glass of beer just to be sociable, so then it might be my turn as well, shortly enough, to find another pub or some high grass on the roadside.

When we finally landed back in to his and Gussie's wee house up on the high road to the Cliffs of Moher, above Doolin near Doonagore, in Luogh North, Micho asked me about the different numbers and letters I had been using which I had found on the map. I showed him the difference between the large N (or National) highways and the smaller county and rural numbered roads, and he said: "Ah, Faith, that's great," and felt it was a great thing to know. I felt happy I could be the one to teach him the bones of map reading after our long journey. A day or so later he brought out a drawing to show me of a map he'd drawn and lettered and colored, and won a prize for in the Doolin School way back in his childhood when he was a "young scholar." It was after that trip that we agreed that he would come to visit me in upstate New York, and I would try to set up some gigs and we'd play it by ear – no pun intended – I really had no idea of what to expect or how this would turn out, but making it happen seemed like a fine idea.

"And into Amerikay"

Back in the States, as luck or serendipity, or both, would have it, around this time my sister-in-law, Neva Winter, a school and town librarian in Rye, NY, at the time, and a founding member of the Rye Storytellers Association, had arranged for a young musician by the name of Bill Ochs to come to the Rye Library and present a demonstration on the tin whistle and the Uilleann Pipes for the public and the library community. She mentioned myself and my adventures with Micho to Bill at that event, and shared copies of my books with him, and related my travels to Doolin, etc. He had been in Ireland many years before and had met Micho briefly, and was delighted to hear of my connection with him. He was also the author of a very successful tin whistle tutor: *The Clarke Tin Whistle Book*. He rang me shortly thereafter and we agreed to try and book gigs for Micho around NYC and Philadelphia, as well as upstate NY, and eventually we also managed to fit in a trip up to Boston.

Meeting Bill brought not only another friend into my life, but also another extremely, meticulous and knowledgeable Irish music scholar, teacher and performer. With his help we set up some incredibly interesting dates for Micho, which also led to a return visit a couple years later. The second visit was primarily centered on Bill's making of a documentary video (and eventually an accompanying CD), The Whistling Ambassador, which includes interviews by Mick Moloney, solo studio sessions, and a concert performance of Micho's in a Church in Greenwich Village. This, along with the previously mentioned "Pure Drop" show, is one of the outstanding video productions about Micho, and that concert footage and the recordings are further testaments that reveal Micho's well-honed craft and professionalism in their vintage maturity.

As the time drew near for Micho's first visit to me in Upstate New York, where I lived in a small village called Cottekill, near the Ulster County Community College campus in Stone Ridge (where we also would hold a concert), I decided to send him a letter of introduction and explanation of his visit and my contact information, etc., to keep with him in case he should need it when travelling, or, God forbid, if he should ever get lost (one of my great fears -- that, and perhaps the breaking of an ankle stepping off a sidewalk in NYC, or some other such dilemma). I was also able to ring Micho on the telephone by that time (1990), as that modern improvement, along with running water and a flush toilet, thanks to Clare County Council grants, had only recently been added to his and Gussie's humble abode far across the Atlantic Ocean. I asked if he had received the Aer Lingus Ticket that we had been kindly given by Brian Scanlon of Aer Lingus, and I suggested he bring about 50 Irish Pounds (this was pre-European Union or Euro days) with him for spending money and safety's sake, and assured him we had lined up some gigs and he wouldn't need for money, or anything else, for that matter.

Well, as the day dawned for his arrival at J.F. Kennedy airport in Queens NY, my dear friend, Dennis Cremmins (RIP), who owned a large comfortable van, and at whose home in Irvington, NY (close to the city and our first few gigs) would be where MIcho would spend his first weekend, and I headed off together to meet and collect him at the airport. Dennis proved to be another key ingredient in making Micho's tour, especially around the metropolitan area and in Westchester County, a great success. Bill Ochs had also done a fabulous job of contacting all of his extensive connections in the New York Irish music scene. These were people I would meet for the first time along with Micho, like: Kathleen Biggins, host of the Fordham University Radio Irish program; Don Meade, who hosted the main Irish venue of the time at the Eagle Tavern on West 14th St., where Micho's first gig was scheduled for that Friday evening; and Earle Hitchner, who wrote Irish Music reviews at that time for the Irish Echo newspaper. Fair play to Earle, he showed up immediately after Micho's arrival to interview him at Dennis and Lois Cremmins' home in Irvington, which was situated on a hill above the east bank of the Hudson River, near Sleepy Hollow, one town south of Tarrytown where the beautiful Tappan Zee Bridge crosses the Hudson.

As I waited for Micho to come through the exit door at the International Arrivals Building that day, it began to dawn on me again (Gus O'Connor's wife, Doll, had already sternly warned me to take good care of him!) that I would be escorting one of Ireland's national treasures around, and God forbid anything should happen to him. And my worry level started to increase as I noticed he wasn't with the last of the stragglers departing the Aer Lingus flight from Shannon. Then I heard my name being paged over the intercom system -- Oh, oh, I thought, this doesn't bode well. I quickly made my way to Customs, and there was Micho, not a bother on him, playing the tin whistle to two young Aer Lingus Attendant/Stewardesses (probably living in Queens or on Long Island, working the ticket counters at JFK), and they with teary eyes saying: "He reminds me so much of my Grandfather, etc.," and who were visibly touched by his mere presence, as many would be later-along on this tour. Truly, I witnessed a good few people break into tears just at the meeting of Micho Russell – even some who never knew or heard of him. He had a cultural presence about him that transcended generations and geography.

I met with the Customs Marshall; a large African-American man with a shiny badge, you see, and asked was there a problem? He explained, not really, but that Mr. Russell didn't have an address with him of where or who he was to end up staying with in America. I suppose he'd left the letter I mailed back home, and I soon found out he had told the Customs Agent that he was going to see: "Dennis Winter. Ah, Faith, I think he lives up by a place called Woodshtock." Only Micho could have imagined they'd let him in to the States with that kind of pure, simple, and yet, perfectly true destination. There are legions of stories and tales (some bawdy, most humorous, some touching) of Micho's travels (and wanderings, as he did occasionally get lost [never for too long] on some folks) in England and Germany and Holland, and of course in his beloved Ireland. One could write and edit a large volume of those collected anecdotes alone. I will try to limit mine to those that happened primarily in my presence and especially on these few trips to America in the 1990s.

As Micho settled in for the weekend at the Cremmins household, a home which was no stranger to music, Dennis having been a fine professional Bass Player and band member in many working groups, and a talented man who genuinely loved and listened to all kinds of music, and also, it didn't hurt (not for nothin'. . .) that he had grown up in an Irish family in Ozone Park. Being a really bright guy, among many other fine attributes, he immediately recognized and knew full-well the value in helping out, and also of exposing his children to a musician and personality the likes of whom will never be seen again: the likes of a Micho Russell; the likes of Dennis' ancient, and not so ancient, rural (Kerry) Irish ancestry. Micho was the likes of someone many of us born in America felt we needed to know, to signify with, to connect us to an Irish past, to an older form of authentic country wisdom, something really real: the real thing. Whatever it was, I'm convinced Micho Russell was indeed a very rare, real-thing individual.

Micho's earnest and relentless curiosity, his exquisite brand of wondering, and his overall inquisitiveness concerning the world about him (and its inhabitants), and his vast, active, and keenly alert memory never ceased to amaze me. It was constantly at work in his life: in the present moment, and then he could also allude to, and reach far into the past; his personal, distant past as if little or no time had elapsed at all; and also into the historical and mythological, legendary, Irish past. He was constantly at work making connections in his folkloric mind; placing the world and its inherent experiences into a framework that has a tune and a title. A title which magically cues ones imagination to visit the name and place and the events of its emotive theme or the balladry of its verses: the folksong, the tune as friend and "brother to the prayer," the lore, the poem. These and the melody, the air and the tune, are really what made him tick. I believe this is also how he configured his world view; refined his worldliness, and how he pursued his personalized form of self-education and musical skill. His development as a player was based on early, and much, rote learning of tunes (melodies) from childhood onward. This, coupled with having to advance along with his equally talented musical brothers, which I'm sure must have kept a certain degree of competiveness alive in the mix, as well as deserved emulation, took a considerable amount of constancy and a disciplined focus over time to achieve the degree of originality and the world-class stature he was eventually awarded in his own lifetime.

Before Earle Hitchner's arrival for the interview on that first full day in America (a Thursday), Dennis and I had been chatting with Micho and listening to him play a few tunes in the kitchen, and our talk came around to the place name: Irvington. "How did it ever get its name?" asks Micho. Well, off we go into the literary realm of Washington Irving and his writings (and re-workings), which are often credited with being the earliest fictional American short stories (Poe actually gets the prize for inventing the form), though granted their roots are easily recognizable as Dutch and Germanic fairytales, to be sure, like: "The Legend of Sleepy Hollow;" "The Headless Horseman;" "Rip Van Winkle;" etc. All are definitely Hudson Valley tales, however, and Micho enjoyed hearing and taking in this sense-of-place info. He also greatly admired the view from above the river there in Irvington, as he took a first stroll around the town on his own. Naturally, he discovered a Tea Shop up the street and of course one of the women working there had Irish relations. Fast friends in the new world: they didn't even charge him for the muffins and tea!

Earle Hitchner did a great interview with Micho and a fine job on the article which came out that following week, and really helped spread the word that a legend was in the area. As I met these people in the New York Irish Music world, such as Earle, I quickly realized they knew their stuff. I had no idea when I went to Ireland to seek out the music that such an extensive, vibrant scene existed in NYC, practically in my own back-yard. In my naivete, I must have thought everyone had left the traditional music back in Ireland when they emigrated. Neither did I know, at that time, of the Irish Folk revival that took place at the same time ours did here in the 1960's, spawning Traditional Super-groups such as: Planxty, the Bothy Band, The Boys of the Lough; and songwriters like Mickey MacConnell, and also, large outdoor Folk Festivals such as the Lisdoonvarna Festival. Through this adventure with Micho Russell, I came to know of and to meet many musicians in Ireland, and ironically, only through him did I learn of New York players such as Lad O'Beirne, Andy McGann, Jack and Fr. Charlie Coen, Felix Dolan, Mike Rafferty over in New Jersey, Mike McHale up in Catskill, NY, etc., and also of the generation born in the New World that followed them, which included young virtuosos such as Brian Conway, Eileen Ivers, and Joanie Madden to name just a few from the New York scene, and such as John Williams and Liz Carroll out in Chicago.

Micho also appeared later that weekend, thanks again to Dennis Cremmins at the wheel of his Plantsman's Van, at the Fordham University radio station studio down in the Bronx on Fordham Road, to meet and be interviewed by Kathleen Biggins for her show: "A Thousand Welcomes." Being the premier traditional Irish music program in the metropolitan area, her broadcast featuring Micho and his music reached an extensive audience. We were all quite pleased when phone calls began to come in from many listeners who either knew Micho back in Ireland before they had emigrated, or knew of his charm and the fame of the Russell Brothers due to their connection to, or interest in, the music and Irish culture in general. Many of these types of fans showed up at his gigs and concerts, and many just called to have a word with Micho. I was amazed at the breadth of some of these connections that were made, and I could see Micho was absolutely delighted to talk to and meet folks he hadn't seen since the 1950s – some he hadn't spoken to since as far back as the 1930s and '40s.

One call came in from a listener in New Jersey, a member of the Paterson, NJ, Historical Society, and it astounded both Bill Ochs and me. The man particularly enjoyed hearing Micho sing his fabulous version of the song: "John Phillip Holland," about the Clare-man: "who invented the sub-ma-rrr-ine." This song, written by Brendán Ó Higgins, a Clare native who now teaches and resides in Boston, MA, first bowled me over when Micho sang it for me back in Doolin. (It is also included in the *Piper's Chair No, 2*, collection) Having been a submarine sailor myself in the 1960's my fondness for this song is understandable. Even more so, considering that my older brother, Ford Winter, was a submariner on the diesel boats out New London, Conn. in the late 1950's, and also, as our father, William E. Winter had been a U.S. Navy hard-hat salvage diver and instructor during WWII, and later on in the 1950's he also worked as a pipe-fitter at Electric Boat (now General Dynamics) in Groton, Conn. building the Nautilus, America's first nuclear powered submarine. The song's popularity among fans and concertgoers soon became evident at each performance. Dennis Cremmins and I thought perhaps we should add a sticker on the cassette cases of the tapes that we were selling for Micho at gigs, which would read: Contains the Hit Single, "John Phillip Holland"

Micho's introduction to this song was always a remarkable bit of stagecraft that varied from show to show, and since the word "show" has popped up, let me say unequivocally, MIcho was indeed a showman. Here in America he proved it nightly. He may have come a long way from his simple, rural farmer's background, but he knew and understood well, the makings and trappings of show business, and he also knew that the music business was a big business. Micho's stardom took wings in New York City and the acclaim that was given him can only have surprised him, but I'm sure it also greatly pleased him.

Naturally, finding out the history of the man from Liscannor whose first submersible torpedo boat, "The Fenian Ram," was tested-out in the Passaic River in Paterson, NJ, and whose surname is indeed on the first commissioned submarine in the U.S. Naval Fleet: The Holland, SS 1 (sub surface #1), was incredible. Even more fantastic was the fact that the man who called-in had also asked us if we knew that the "Fenian Ram," Holland's first prototype, was still in existence and was in fact housed in a museum in Paterson? We were simply delighted beyond expectations to hear of this, and I quickly arranged to borrow my sister-n-law's big comfortable Pontiac station wagon, pick up Bill Ochs along the way, and take Micho to Patterson to see the boat later that week. Again, this is a fine example of the type of folkloric connection that Micho's life evolved and revolved around.

I had also received in the post at that time, sent by the Historical Society, a photo-copy excerpt from Holland's biography; written, I think, by his son, and which is an in-depth discussion of Holland's attempts to design, build and sell his idea to the U.S. Department of the Navy. A must read for submarine *aficianados*, at any rate, and Micho sang that song at almost all of his concerts here in the States to great, warm, and resounding applause. His introduction to that song is also a good example of how meaningful these connections of "air" (as in "slow air" or melody) and verse --the sociological import of the story—were to him; as was who composed it, how it was written, and how he came to have it in his repertoire. This song particularly showcased his pride and fondness for its relevance to his native County Clare: "So raise your glass in the air, for the man from Clare, who invented the sub-marine." It is indeed a classic Irish folk-ballad and Mr. Ó'Higgins deserves every high mark and credit for authoring such a fine example of the Irish historical ballad genre, and also for skillfully crafting ones ballad in a specifically traditional manner to suit and fit an early air (melody) that particularly suits the mood of the song. It's a topper!

On the night of the Eagle Tavern gig, we left Irvington in Dennis' van and headed south into Manhattan – deep into the heart of New York City. Since we were driving in a van with commercial license plates (tags) down to the gig, which was way down in lower Manhattan at West 14th street, I felt badly that Micho would miss seeing a better view of the skyline that other avenues of approach would have afforded. It was also in the late fall of the year, and dusk was descending early as we drove down through the Bronx, then Harlem, then the upper East side, then through Mid-town traffic snarls, and then over to the Lower West Side, finally arriving to a cold, windy sidewalk in what was then still a meat-packing, trucking and industrial area of lower Manhattan at 14th street and 10th Ave. Most of 14th street was a long-time commercial, east-west thoroughfare, and which, though it was just turning towards gentrification at that time, still harbored creatures of the underbelly there on the far West End, and to my dismay on that particular night, cold as it was, there were still a few streetwalkers, Ladies of the Evening, so to speak, standing bare-legged on the opposite side-walk as we approached the curb in front of the club. "Where will the poor girls sleep?" was Micho's heartfelt query, voiced in that truly concerned tone of voice with the big, soft Clare accent, and I could only shake my head and say: "I haven't a clue, Micho, but it's a sad place, no doubt."

After that long arduous drive, bouncing down through many of the darker scenes one might wish to see, or not see, in NYC, I recall the next day Micho asking me: "Do you suppose there are some rough places in New York?" Well, I supposed there were, and I was still disappointed I hadn't been able to show Micho the lights of Broadway and the Theater District, or manage to catch a good view of the Skyline. That would come later, though, and especially on the second tour when Bill Ochs would take him for a ferry-cruise around the island on the Circle Line, and also for a double-decker bus tour around the city. When I finally did get a good sky-scraper view one afternoon later on, parked somewhere on the West Side up nearer mid-town, he looked up and said: "Wouldn't it be terrible if the bombs fell here?" I least expected this response, but then I hadn't lived through the Second World War (the Emergency, in Ireland) as did Micho when he was a young man, and he would have known intimately about the London Blitz from his parent's and their generation when he was a child, experiences that obviously had affected him and were still with him. It is also an eerily prophetic statement, when looking back from here as a New Yorker in the post 9/11 era.

That night at the Eagle Tavern, as we entered the front door of the Pub's bar-room, which had a great, real-old-time New York, shamrock-bar feel to it, we were met and led by Bill Ochs to the back room, which was just off the performance hall area. This was separated from the bar area by a desk-lit, reservation podium, and staffed by a volunteer receptionist/ticket-taker, and we were all pleasantly surprised at the turnout – a packed house!

The stage in that listening room was back-dropped by a truly wonderful, full-sized wall mural of a turn-of- the century, working man's New York Harbor scene. The atmosphere it created, along with the spot-lit chair and microphone at center stage on a painted, hardwood floor, set one immediately back into the Vaudeville era of Manhattan, with its vast history and countless numbers of shows and performers. One might easily imagine seeing one of the early, professional Irish Minstrels (remember also they were the first to do "blackface"), such as Dan Emmett, who introduced the 5-string banjo accompaniment to the New York stage (it is said that he's also credited with having penned "Dixie"); or perhaps a recital from the likes of the great Uilleann Piper, Patsy Touhey; or some pure Irish Tenor, singing "Mother *Mo Chroi*." Micho couldn't have fit the role more perfectly, and his show that night was impeccably performed and filled and infused with Micho's magnanimity, humor and skill.

Don Meade, another active reviewer and critic(for The Irish Voice, at that time), and a key person in the NY Irish Music Scene (much like the previously mentioned Biggins and Hitchner), is a man well-versed and much-practiced at gracefully and knowledgeably presenting star-quality players to extremely keen, and fairly (for lack of a better term) sophisticated audiences, and he presented Micho that night in the warmest and most-welcoming manner to an audience of avid, metropolitan-area, lovers of Irish traditional music and folk culture. The evening was a tremendous success.

With our first packed-house under our belts, and with the many rave-up comments and the heartfelt ringing of applause from those fortunate enough to have ventured out that evening still echoing in our ears, Dennis, Micho and I headed home to Irvington with great laughs and smiles. Bill Ochs literally tin-whistled his way up the sidewalks along the west-side, back north to his mid-town pad, with a great renewed sense of the magnificence of the humble Pennywhistle. Things were looking up -- from then on, that was pretty much the story: people got word that Micho was in America, and wherever we went, we had full capacities attending each event. Some audience members were Irish music lovers, some were novice- enthusiasts, and some simply were old friends and acquaintances from back in Ireland who were now living near any one of our concerts and gigs. These appearances ranged as far south as Washington DC, and from Philadelphia, PA, on up to Upstate New York, and as far north as Boston, Mass.

Micho was definitely much more well-known in America than he could have ever imagined; of this I'm sure, and it was truly heartwarming to see some of these reunions and to be a part of all the incredible connections that were being made along the way on this folkloric journey. Since neither Bill nor I were experienced promoters, or in any way connected with the business of booking and publicizing artists, we began to relax a bit and enjoyed the days and nights that followed with a growing feeling of security that we would likely be able to not only pull this off, but also send Micho home with a good, solid professional paycheck.

The following day was open —no gigs or interviews. We'd been going flat-out from the moment the plane landed. Micho enjoyed the day off, and relaxed at the Cremmins' apartment in Irvington. Later in the day he made his way back to the Tea Shop for a brief visit and chat, and didn't he then also take a notion to walk on up the block and drop in to the Public Library -- on his own; and didn't he then return home with a huge leather-bound volume on the life of Washington Irving tucked under his arm. We asked how in the world he managed to come home with this marvelous, valuable tome? It turns out, he'd gone in and said to the librarian: "I'm very interested in this man, Washington Irving," and was there a book? Which he was duly given and entrusted with, without having a loaner's card, or for that matter, a definite local address and I doubt they even asked his name. I imagine he may have mentioned Dennis Cremmins, but we were just floored by this determined effort to put the folklore of place in perspective: he was relentless at building this accumulated sense of understanding through regional folklore – in whatever region he may have found himself.

As we looked forward to the next, upcoming weekend concert at the Rye Arts Center, in Rye, NY, Micho had some brief days off that week and was able to fit in a reunion with his cousin, Theresa O'Dea, and spend a night out on Long Island at her and her husband, Klaus Hein's home in Massapequa. Our next gig was later on in the mid-week when we would go out that way, collect him, and head nearby to play for an Ancient Order of Hibernian's branch in Bayshore, also on Long Island. Along the way we crammed in a Deli stop, for teas and coffees to-go, with fabulous chicken-salad sandwiches on fresh hard-rolls, which we ate in the van in the parking lot. Micho thought "the salad sandwich was lovely." You can't beat a good NY Deli when you're hungry, can you now?

The next night we played a pub-gig at the Tara Restaurant in Yonkers. Gus Hayes was the owner and had come to America from Ennistymon in Clare, not far from Doolin. He and Micho knew each other well, and Micho brought out an ingenious funny song that night called, "Ennistymon Town" in honor of Gus. Although it is included in the *Piper's Chair No.2* collection, I had never actually heard him sing it. Needless to say, it was a big hit with Gus and his clientele, and Micho performed it as if he had been rehearsing it all week, and probably hadn't sung it in many, many years.

That night was attended by many members of the local *Comhaltas* branch there in Yonkers, headed by a man named Jim McGinty (at the time), and he had arranged for Brian Conway, the popular and well-known NY-Sligo style fiddler, to open the show. That was my first time seeing Brian play, and I was quite struck by his exquisite bowing technique. That group of *aficionados* at the Tara enjoyed his set and then poured their welcome out for Micho, and his performance, again, was exquisite, relaxed and full of fun, and his amazing cast of songs and tunes continued to please and amaze us all.

Dennis and I were often met with some degree of suspicion at these various events, when people in these rather tightly-knit Irish Music cliques realized that their nearly mythological, Micho Russell (one of the famous Russell Brothers), was showing up with the likes of us? Who in "hell's blue blazes" (to borrow a term from Packie Russell) were these guys, and how did they manage to be the ones bringing Micho to the States? We just kept our cards close to the vest and simply enjoyed our little magical mystery tour, and concentrated on keeping Micho safe and happy. And, as I was extremely intent on learning the music, I tried to concentrate my focus there; trying to absorb every note I possibly could on those fine nights and moments when Micho's whistle or big-timber flute sent them out; delivered always with his own pure brand of Irishness (whatever that might be . . .), and his unique, specifically Gaelic lilt of phrasing and allure, into the enchanted evenings.

The concert at the Rye Arts Center, on Milton Road, had been organized by Neva Winter and her colleague, Judy Greenfield, who were founding members of the Rye Storytellers Association; the sponsor of the event, and who were ever after referred to as "the girls from the Rye College." That night is particularly memorable for several reasons: firstly that it was the most formal recital setting we'd so far encountered; and secondly, it was attended by several key audience members who also lent a special quality to the evening.

As the hall was filling, an interesting, well-dressed and bright looking couple, Hartley ("Bob") and Michele Barclay, introduced themselves to me. They had also brought an old friend of theirs along from Iona College, a Brother Quinn, another Ennistymon native and a Gaelic speaker. In our brief meeting there in the foyer, the Barclays told me of their plans to build a home in Doolin to retire to. They had been in Clare recently and fallen in love with it, and had decided on a pure, spur-of-the-moment whim, and with a breath of divine inspiration thrown in for good measure, to buy a site of land on the hillside above Doolin not far from Micho's old house and birthplace, and to head there for their retirement years. I thought this was interesting and serendipitous, and wished them well, but thought I might have heard talk of plans and dreams of going back to Ireland like this before. However, It all came definitely true, and over the next decade or more we became the greatest of friends as over the ensuing years I accepted their gracious hospitality and often visited and stayed with them up in Luogh, on many, many visits.

Before Micho and I went on stage that night in Rye, and as well at many of these gigs and concerts, I usually asked if he'd like a drop of the warm stuff? I made it a point to keep a small bottle of brandy with us for these moments; to loosen up the nerves a bit, like. Neither Micho nor I were what you might call drinkers – far from it, but usually he would indeed have a small sup, but this night he declined for some reason. Well, I had my own small sup and went on-stage anyway, sang a few songs, played my guitar, and then introduced and brought on the star of the evening. Again, Micho didn't fail to impress and enchant this audience; not just with his music, but by his special stage presence alone. If a character like him could be taken for granted back in Ireland, here in the States, I can tell you, he was a rarity that most have never experienced. Those who did attend these concerts were genuinely grateful for the opportunity to experience this extremely entertaining and interesting individual with the somehow endearing quality about him.

Backstage during the intermission, I asked Micho how he was doing and he said: "Maybe I will have a drop [of the brandy] after all. That wasn't a priest out there at all, only a Christian Brother!" You can't make this stuff up, dear reader. He was just a joy and surprise at every turn and at any turn of phrase as well. We went back on to close the show and received many visitors back-stage after the concert was over, including the Barclays and Brother Quinn. I recall a young, obviously well-educated journalist coming back to meet Micho that night, and she asked him this question: "What is, or do you have, your own philosophy, Mr. Russell?" As he was often wont to do (even on-stage, to deflect any possible dead-air time), Micho took a good, long, pregnant pause, all the while shaking the whistle a bit as he was thinking, and then replied softly and sincerely: "Just, . . . keep going."

One professional musician in attendance that evening was Abe Silverman, who also came back to meet and congratulate us. A well-known, working Jazz woodwind player and composer, active on the NY scene and also a career public school music teacher, Abe commented to me that Micho had perfect, as if classically trained, "finger posture" for flute-playing, and also expressed how much he had enjoyed the evening. We all enjoyed these events; practicing musicians and non-playing listeners alike.

That night after the show we moved Micho's base-camp and he was put up at my brother's house nearby. Ford was just nearing retirement from his career as the Physical Education Director and Swimming and Diving Coach at the nearby Hommocks School, in Mammaronek, NY, and as mentioned, his wife Neva was still a working Library Arts Specialist at the Milton School. Micho fit in playing a daytime concert for the children there, as he also did for Lois and Dennis Cremmins' daughters, Betty and Loretta, at their school in Mt.Kisco, NY. (Naturally he played his version of "The Maids of Mt. Cisco" up there for them). We would also leave out from the Winter's house there in Rye when we took our jaunt out to Paterson, NJ, to see J. P. Holland's boat.

After meeting Micho briefly that next morning and while excusing himself to Micho as he headed out to work on either boat or automobile (which he's often at), my brother used a phrase he'd picked up on one of his many journeys down South, to North Carolina, chasing leads on collectible cars and the like: "Well, I guess I've got to 'step up to the plow' now, so I'll see you lads later." Before he'd hardly left the room, Micho said to me: "There's a lot of meaning in them words, you know." That phrase quickly became part of Micho's vocabulary, to be sure. I also asked him what he thought of my brother in general: "He's a very fit man," he replied.

After that long, rewarding, initial week in America, we next welcomed Micho up to the Mid-Hudson Valley to my house in Cottekill, NY. He had met my wife, Ellen, previously when we were on a holiday trip together to Ireland some years before, but it was his first meeting with my son Stephen, 9 (at the time), my step-son Luke (14), and my older son, from my first marriage, Travis (19), who came down from Ithaca, NY, for the occasion. I was thrilled they could all meet Micho -- who would stay with us there in Cottekill through the Thanksgiving Holiday that year, and we would perform at several venues in the area and continue to meet up with old friends from back in Ireland; then we would manage to venture out to Philadelphia to see Mick Moloney, and Micho would also spend a weekend in Washington DC at the home of friends who had met him back in Doolin, Bob and Susan Meehan. They had contacted me by phone about the possibility of Micho coming down to do a house concert and to be shown the sights. We also ventured up to Saratoga Springs to play a pub-gig at The Parting Glass, and also appeared on Jay Ungar and Molly Mason's radio program, "Dancing on the Air," on WAMC, a National Public Radio station in Albany, NY.

Somewhere along in here we made it up to see Jimmy Scales at his Woodstock Pub. Jimmy was partly responsible for my going to Ireland in the first place and for directing me specifically to his home-town of Doolin. He had left Doolin when he was still a teenager, first to London but then on to join up and work with his older brother, Pappy, in the bar trade in the Bronx. After marrying, Jimmy and his wife, Maureen, ended up buying their own pub upstate in Woodstock, the only Irish Pub there in those days which was a great local for many Ulster County residents. His reunion with Micho was full of laughs and great stories from back as far as the 1940s. Jimmy recounted walking miles and miles to house dances in his youth, sometimes arriving to find no girls had ventured out, and the lads proceeded to dance "buck-sets" anyway. They weren't about to be deprived of a night's fun over the one detail. I thought this was a good example of how important and how much a part of the intrinsic fabric of social life in rural Ireland, folk music and set-dancing was. Just as importantly, it was something which the Russell Brother's lives from their youths through middle-age had revolved around entirely.

At some point in the night at Jimmy Scales's, Jim proceeded to ask Micho a rather touchy kind of question about some shady, infamous event, something that had happened way in the past, and he wondered about the outcome and if there had been a court trial? Micho's cool reply was: "Well, I don't know much about that, now, but I'd say the man was disqualified in the finish-up." Micho wouldn't be one to spend much time on any talk that leaned towards the bawdy or unseemly, or gossipy. I was also minding Micho closely that night, as I was my own self, for when you fell in with Jimmy it could be a long night, and I was driving. So, we said our goodnights before it got too late and headed back down the road to Cottekill.

While at my house there in the late upstate autumn, which was somewhat more of a relaxed and rural setting than he'd been in so far, Micho enjoyed his walks around the neighborhood, and one of the first things I saw him do out in the small field behind my garage and sheds was to take hold of an old, full-sized scythe I had leaning against the tool-shed and go give a lash to some tall, standing grass out back. Inspired, I went and got the sharpening stone out to give the blade a quick lick. He enjoyed tossing an American football around with the kids in the yard, too, and I dare say the photos of him with it in his hands are probably quite a rarity.

We also introduced him to our neighbor, Pat Flannery, who had emigrated from Porturlin, on the far northwestern coast of County Mayo, many years before (in the 1950's) as a very young man, and after joining the U.S. Army stayed on as a citizen. He and his American-born wife enjoyed having Micho over for tea, and also took him to Mass at our local Catholic Church, St. Peter's, down the hill from us in Rosendale. Pat shared with me how Micho had asked him if he didn't miss Ireland, and how had he managed to adjust to staying here in the States? MIcho's mind was always at work on concerns like this, and we sensed he too was falling a bit in love with America. The Flannery's were a big help to us, keeping an eye out and welcoming Micho over during the day, as I was either working at my carpentry, or attending classes at the University College at New Paltz, trying to complete my late-in-life degrees, and my wife was a full-time nurse at the Kingston City Hospital, and we were also mainly concerned then with raising the kids.

On one of those days, after I had headed off to work early, Ellen had plans to take Micho over to Stephen's elementary school in Rosendale to meet the music teacher, and for him to play a small recital for the children. When Micho asked these gatherings of school children if any were Irish, every hand in the room shot up. The teachers were all extremely grateful to us for bringing Micho into their schools. Kids simply adored him and were always entranced when his tunes were on the air. Unlike in Ireland, many of these children would have never seen or heard an Irish tin whistle and the music it could make.

Before Ellen and Micho were to leave the house that morning and head over to the school, which wasn't very far from our house, Micho caught a brain-wave and decided to "clean the oul' flute." He asked Ellen if she knew if I had any piece of cloth or anything out in my studio/shop to do the job with? She unknowingly found something she thought might work: my saxophone cleaner, which was basically a too-large pad of cloth on a long string, which Micho proceeded to reef and strong-arm up into the old timber flute, where it remained jammed for the next hour or so.

My poor wife was in a panic, calling the school and the music teacher and music stores in Kingston, our nearest small city, and finally, by using a long pointed pair of scissors, managed to snip and snip and finally cut and pick out the infernal obstruction. My wife calmed down a bit, but they still had to hurry over to the school just in time to make the scheduled appointment. Micho would surely have gone over to that school with only his whistle and gotten by without giving a second thought about the flute, I suspect. However, when I returned home that evening he met me out in the yard with this greeting: "I think I drove your wife distracted with the flute."

Back in the house at the dinner table, where we were having Thanksgiving leftovers, I heard the whole story of the day, replete with great intensity and occasional chuckles which I found quite amusing. After they described clearing the flute with the scissors and finally removing the blockage, we had a great laugh after Micho added: "Well, it was a bit of a prostate operation, all right." He knew he was in a nurse's company, too, the divil. Before we finished dinner, he asked if he could have "another small cut of the pumpkin pudding? 'Tis lovely," he added. He had never had pumpkin pie, a main dessert staple for our traditional New England Thanksgiving dinners. He also enjoyed the red-skinned potatoes we'd been having, boiled or mashed, and had commented that he thought they were exceptional spuds. New tastes to try and many new faces to meet over in the New World: Micho was obviously enjoying his visit.

Shortly thereafter, our next major excursion was to Philadelphia, and this was another ramble filled with more incredible folkloric moments, both large and small. Of course Micho had known Mick Moloney many years ago in Ireland; and also when Mick was in London with his first folk-group, The Johnstons (with Paul Brady). He was the first to bring Micho to London to tour with them. Down in Philly, Mick (who was at work on his Doctoral dissertation at the time) held a second, honorary Thanksgiving Dinner for Micho, there at his house in Germantown. The following day Micho gave a master class there to an eager group of tin whistlers (mostly), but a few other players and enthusiasts attended as well, including the fiddler, Kitty Kelley. Micho then performed a concert held at a fabulous, large, hall-like music store, Vintage Instruments, that fairly well reeked of old Philadelphia Irish music history; and which had the largest collection of timber flutes I'd ever seen, as well as a wall full of fiddles. After the gig, we headed south of Philly to a place called Media, PA, for a weekend's visit with a piper friend of Bill's by the name of Roy Rogers. No relation to Dale's husband and happy trails-mate, but an avid piper and a truly wonderful guy; and he and his wife took great care of us at their fine big home where we spent a full Sunday relaxing.

First thing that morning, though, I took Micho out into unknown suburban Pennsylvania territory that I had never been in, to find a Mass. He never missed Mass while with us in America. After lunch we lounged a while and chatted with the Rogers' and their friends, and then, lo-and-behold, a mystery phone call came in for "Micho Russell," and it was from someone way out in the Mid-west -- in Chicago, no less. How that man out there ever heard of Micho's whereabouts and was able to actually track us down and phone us at Roy's (on a Sunday) is still a wonder to me. But he did, and Micho had a great chat with an old friend, via a handheld, wireless telephone, and at the finish-up of their conversation they were discussing a questionable goal that was scored by one side or the other in some football match held back in Clare some 60 years ago in the 1930s.

We lingered in Philly that evening, awaiting word on whether or not the Clancy Brothers (due to start a U.S. tour) would be landing in town in time for us to meet them before we headed back up north to New York State. We'd about given up on that idea when Mick called us at the last moment and gave us directions to the guest cottage the Clancys would be staying at, and to inform us that their plane had just landed and that they would be there by the time we drove up to call in to them, somewhere on the North side of the city. As I finally found the neighborhood, and drove up the small residential street looking for the correct address, there, out in the front yard, waiting for Micho to arrive, was Paddy Clancy, the eldest brother of the group at that time, and with a shirt and tie on from the flight. They were all amazed to meet Micho here in the U. S. They gave him a great welcome and plenty of advice about being sure to "get his money," and being careful and all, while touring the States; and we proceeded to have an incredible night with the Clancys.

They had just come from their brother Tommy's funeral that fall, back in Carrick-on-Suir, and were definitely still in a kind of wake-mode: one story after another from Liam, then Bobby, then Paddy -- you couldn't get a word in edgewise; and these stories were full of humor, history, irony, you name it; all the elements of good true storytelling were at work that evening. We had great laughs with them, and we also didn't mind that the kitchen in the guest house had been fully catered for their arrival either. It was a long, fantastic night, and finally, on the drive home, Micho commented on how struck by, and how pleasing it was for him, "to see the brothers getting along so well." I think this kind of warm *camaraderie* was not as evident between the Russell brothers for the most part. They seemed to come and go, each on their own paths, without too much concern about what the others might be up to. This was true, I'm sure, of many such teams of bachelor brothers who ended up living together in their family's farmhouse, not always out of a specific desire to do so, but because things simply turned out that way.

It was nearly day-break by the time we arrived back in Ulster County that next morning, just in time for me to head to work (ugh . . .) and for Micho to rest up a day or two with us back in Cottekill. Around the time of Micho's arrival, I had written and sent copies of my books over to Pete Seeger, who lives in Beacon, NY, across the Hudson on the east bank, and south of us by about 20 or 30 miles. I was thrilled one morning that week when I received a letter from him asking me to ring him up and make plans to bring Micho over for lunch at his house when we could. I promptly followed up and had a marvelous, extremely memorable conversation on the phone with Pete Seeger that ranged from settling on a day on which to visit, to a lengthy musicological discussion concerning Seeger's father's (a composer and musicologist) attempt to introduce the term, "en-periodic cadence," to denote the unmetered time of the pause in Irish, slow-air playing, into the canon of music composition and notational terms. Unfortunately, Pete added, it wasn't taken up by the literati of the day.

Pete then launched into an anecdote about how Alan Lomax, the pre-eminent American folklore collector, had been talking (by telephone) with a fellow folklore enthusiast living way up in Northern Scotland, who had been lately listening via shortwave ("ham") radio, to folk music from Mongolia. He told Lomax that what he liked about it was its, "high lonesome sound." This, ironically, is a term which Seeger's half-brother, Mike, has usually been given credit for having coined in describing some of the music of his Appalachian environs, and in particular, sounds like those achieved by Bill Monroe and the Bluegrass Boys, or say, the Louvin Brothers.

Well, we agreed on a day and time to visit, and Pete ended our conversation with this sentiment: "Let your mind wander over this, Dennis. Pythagoras thought he had it all figured out, but Pi threw him for a loop!" Needless to say, Pete Seeger is an interesting guy, and I explained to Micho a bit about his incredible contributions to the world of folk music and also his pioneering efforts, including the building of the authentic Sloop, *The Clearwater*, and the ensuing environmental movement that began to clean up the Hudson River, and by extension, the interdependent ecology of our entire Hudson Valley region – an amazing and heroic feat, to say the least. I think Micho already vaguely knew that Pete was also a world-famous folk singer, and he had met many such figures along the way, but I could tell he was elated with meeting a man who struck him personally as a truly distinguished, important figure. Less than a week later, as he introduced a tune or song during one part of his performance, Micho mentioned he'd just recently met a man named, "Pete **See**- -gerr, and I found him to be a very interesting man, you see . . ." And, on with the show . . . .

Our luncheon that day at the Seeger's was definitely another folkloric highlight – you can imagine how elated I was as I sat between two patriarchs of the folk-music world, representing folk cultures from both sides of the Atlantic, as they chatted and we all enjoyed the homemade fare that Pete's wife, Toshi, had prepared.

One humorous moment (for me, anyhow) occurred when a large, tall, lathe-turned, wooden pepper-grinder made its way 'round the table and ended up in Micho's hands. I could see the bewilderment on his face, as if he was saying to himself: "What in the world is this yoke all about, anyhow . . . ?" I quickly took hold of it, saying, "Here, let me see that, Micho," gave a quick twist of pepper onto his soup, and passed it on to Pete. As usual: "Faith, that's great," was Micho's undeterred response, sounded along with a chuckle.

After lunch we moved into the living room, and Pete and Micho tuned up, found a few tunes to play together, including a fairly tight and snappy version of "The Irish Washerwoman." And Pete also spent some time truly enjoying just sitting there listening to Micho's whistle playing. At some point during this session, Micho commented, once again, on the view: Pete's home sits high on a hill above the river and looks out on a bay near Newburgh and affords a view of the Hudson Highlands near West Point to the south. Micho said it reminded him of a song called: "The Trip I took Over the Mountain," and that he was sorry, but that he also had the words "all lost." Pete said it was funny he should mention that song because, in the 1950's, it turns out, he had employed an Irish carpenter who worked on finishing the roof of the barn for him, and that that man used to sing that song. He added that he could probably find the lyrics and would post them over to me. Micho was pleased to hear this and quipped, "There's a lot of men in Clare 'would like to have them words." I thought this a nice natural example of how valued an old tune or song-lyric is to those who prize them. Pete also asked me to send him the lyrics of Richard Fariňa's song, "Love is Lord of All," written to the air of "My Lagan Love."

Fair-play to Pete Seeger for entertaining our visit that day, and for, indeed, following up and sending us a hand-written copy of the song, including the music staff and notation. He's a man who has an enormous pile of correspondence sitting beside his desk, and he tries to respond to all comers when and if he can, and I was genuinely grateful for the time he took to make Micho's visit upstate even more eventful than I could have imagined. He also ended our visit out in the yard, as we headed to my car, with a heartfelt farewell and this: "I could listen to you all day, Micho Russell. Safe travels!"

I relinquished my duties as *charge d'affaires* for Mr. Russell shortly after that luncheon, for a few days anyhow, as Micho flew to Washington, DC, unaccompanied (and I had my worries you can bet), to meet up with his friends, the Meehans. They collected him at the airport and really showed Micho a great time in the Capitol, visiting the monuments and the grand mall, holding a House-concert and master-class at their home, and caring royally for their special guest, "the whistling ambassador."

On the evening I was to re-unite with him and collect him at the Albany Airport, we were booked in Saratoga Springs for a gig at the Cohan's, Parting Glass Pub. I was concerned he might be knackered-out and a bit weary from all the travel, etc, until I saw him come beaming through the landing gate, sporting a huge grin and wearing a brand new, black sweatshirt with a huge red-white-and blue bedecked American Bald Eagle across the chest, and "Washington DC" scrolled beneath it. He was as happy as I'd ever seen him and was rarin' to go do the gig, and even played a late-lasting session after his show that night. I hope I have that kind of steam and pluck when I reach my mid-seventies, as was the case for Micho at the time.

A day or two after that long night, one more long night on the road, we played a big concert at Ulster County Community College, just up the hill from my house on Cottekill Road, in Stone Ridge. I was particularly responsible for arranging this concert and had been looking forward to it with great anticipation. I had coordinated this with the College Association and with Dr. Richard Olsen, chairman of the Music Department, whom I had studied with, and had sung for in the College Chorus under his conductor's direction back in the late 70s. A wonderful musician and composer himself, Dr. Olsen immediately recognized how special and beneficial it would be to have Micho perform for the Community and for the music students at an afternoon master-class. Both events were filmed by the College Audio-Visual department, and the evening concert raised a considerable amount of money for a student scholarship fund. It was the largest, standing-room-only turnout the College had ever had up to that point. Dr. Olsen and Micho had gotten on great together, and his presentation for the students that afternoon was a special moment for all of us. Micho had a knack for communicating to musical novices and enthusiasts how the music worked in him, for him, and through him for audiences. He was inspirational to struggling players and to listeners, by his personal references to the tunes and songs, reminding them that these tunes are also companions and one can "get great imaginations" from them. Micho had much akin with the true storytellers of old, especially as regards his singing, the best of whom re-lived the stories as they told them.

He also rose from his chair during the demonstration and danced a good blast of *sean nos* (old style) dance steps for them which was one of the only times in America he was filmed doing so. Micho also related to me, around this time, how lucky he felt to have the music to be involved with in his later years in life – how he gained great comfort and a sense of companionship by having the music in his life.

He proudly wore his new sweatshirt for the concert that night, and after I warmed them up with a few Appalachian ballads and guitar pieces, he came on and truly presented a magnificent show. The room was stunned by his originality and authentic presence, and he warmed and regaled that large crowd with his beautifully delivered playing and his seemingly-simple approach to traditional Irish music.

That night, as he introduced his version of "Drowsy Maggie – in an old fashioned way. . .," that he usually played on the "big timber" flute, he explained how: "Somehow or other, over the years, the tin whistle has become my instrument. To be playing the timber flute you'd want to be practicing it a lot, to have the breath, you see." "And," he added, "You'd also want to have your own teeth." Well, a huge laugh erupted with that offering, and to be sure, Micho had a great chuckle at himself and a good laugh along with the audience. It is an important quality of distinction to find in a man, and perhaps more so in a musician, a person who can truly have a laugh at himself, especially in today's competitive scene and world. You can also believe me when I tell you it wasn't too far down the road, at some other show, that Micho used that introduction again, all the more to the benefit of his stage-craft.

Another similar, introductory anecdote we heard that evening was one that Micho often used when introducing an American tune that he played called, "The Arkansas Traveler." He usually stumbled a bit with the title, and still had a bit of difficulty pronouncing the name of that state, and he usually took the literal route (why wouldn't you?), and it came out: "Arkan –sass." He also occasionally introduced a tune called "The Little Black Pig," with this particularly American anecdote, as well.

That tale, as Micho had it, goes: that there was a boat-wreck one time, on the Mississippi River near St. Louis, and a whole cargo of pigs (*bon'eens* and *bonhams*) were lost overboard and many had drowned.

When those that had died were all collected on shore, you see, there was a pyre built and they were all burnt-up in a huge, big fire. Micho assured us that it was supposed to have been the "first barbecue in America." That Ulster County Community College concert turned out to be an extremely rewarding folklore event; another great success and night to remember; another great night ramblin' with Micho Russell.

These ramblings in America on this first tour were also drawing nearer to a close, and Micho had a decision to make concerning how he was to spend his last week with us here in the States. He had two options: the first was to follow an invitation to play at McGurks, in St. Louis, where Micho had already been once before, many years earlier, when Joe Burke, the great accordion player was based there. Doing so would involve another round-trip air flight and little or no time back in New York before leaving for home. This would have all been paid for, of course, but I just didn't sense that he was all that keen to go, plus, he'd already been there. He decided on the second option, which was to go to Boston instead.

I had fielded another call from out of the blue at the start of the tour from a man by the name of Gerry Dunleavy. He introduced himself over the phone as a builder in the Boston area, but explained further that he had grown up in Doolin, and of course knew Micho, and said he would love to have us come to Boston and play for the Clare Association up there, which has a large, active membership, and that it would be a benefit for the Down Syndrome Congress. This seemed to suit Micho and me perfectly, and as it turns out was the wise choice for Micho. He had a wonderful reunion-filled time up there in Boston. After further discussion with Dunleavy on the phone that night, it became clear that I was already a friend of his Uncle's, "Brud" (P.J.) Petty; another interesting native Doolin character and farmer whom I had met back in Clare several years previous. Micho also had relatives in Boston that he now looked forward to seeing again, and, overall, it just felt like the right road to take.

So, off we go up to Boston in my old '72 Buick, which had been handed down to me from my dear mother, Dottie, in California, still alive at that time, who'd already put 200,000 or more miles on it since she bought it new. Micho and I cruised up the Interstate in great style, good form, and in good humor.

We stopped for lunch somewhere north of Hartford, Connecticut, where a big strong-looking, heavy-set-but-handsome waitress served us. Micho commented that, "she was a great block of a woman," which was the first time I ever heard that phrase. In Micho's youth that would have passed as a compliment – sturdy women were considered good matches for a farmer to wed back then -- but if one were to use that epithet today I suppose one might get his own block knocked off, eh?

The concert and dance up there in Massachusetts was held at a hall in Saugus, MA, not far from the Dunleavy's home in Winchester, just north of Boston City, and it was another solid success; and a night poignantly filled with the joys (and many tears of joy, as well) of many glad reunions. After Micho performed, Tommy Kierce's ceilli band played for a full dance floor, filled with Clare folks who definitely knew their music and their dances, and certainly hadn't left their fondness or their skills for them back home in Ireland. I was quite taken and surprised by the prominence of Clare accents there that night – you'd have easily thought you were back in Ireland, and specifically in County Clare. They all knew, or knew of, the Russell Brothers, and MIcho was feted well. The Dunleavys took great care of us at their first home on Pilgrim Ave, and during the late-night kitchen session of tea and drinks and chatting till the wee hours it dawned on me that I was having some kind of *déjà vu* moment, or as Yogi Berra might say: "It was like déjà vu all over again." It seemed to me I had heard of these people before: Gerry (who had had a broken leg not that long ago) and his brother, P.J., the carpentry contractors, Toni, Gerry's wife, the Montessori School-teacher and proprietor; and John, their first-born son who was already absolutely totally smitten with traditional music and already loved Micho Russell from watching him on a Doolin video. It seemed I had heard all this before, and I had in fact done so at Gerry's sister's B&B in Doolin. Their Uncle Brud had directed me there one night in the past (Brud and I did some ramblin' around Clare together, too), to book-in with his niece, "Small Mary" (as opposed to "Big Mary," Brud's sister, the mother of Gerry, P.J., Mary and Maurice). She had told me the whole story of her brothers in America, long before, one morning at her breakfast table in the Roadford section of Doolin. It's a small world indeed, especially considering that since then, over the intervening years, I've become close friends with the Dunleavys and no stranger to the Boston traditional music scene either.

A reception room off the main hall was the setting for Micho's reunion with his cousin, Catherine ("Kitty"), d'Entremont; her brother, Tom Clair, and his wife, Mary; and their daughter, Kitty's neice, Kathleen Clair. Micho hadn't ever met Tom, as he was born in America and hadn't ever met Micho. Everyone was amazed that Micho knew he must be Tom Clair because of his Moloney looks! Tom stated to his sister that he felt Micho was, "a very disciplined musician."

Micho amazed us often with this skillful trait of remembering the names and recognizing the faces of people he may have met anywhere and everywhere. I believe this was also one of Micho's greatest sources of personal joy: the pure meeting and beholding of the face, name and personality of another magical human being. He was deeply aware of the spiritual goodness and beauty of another pilgrim's soul and the possible complexity of their being; he was keenly and sincerely interested in who and what they were about. And I know he was delighted to meet Kitty, his musical cousin, in Boston.

Relatives aside, Micho met many other friends that night from back in Ireland both young and old. Brendán Ó Higgins was there, the author of the submarine song, "John Phillip Holland," and now a teacher in the Boston area, as was Alfie Crowe from Ennistymon, a right character and full of fun, much like Cyril Kilderry, who was also there. Mike Shannon, a cousin of Paddy Shannon's from Fisher Street was there; as was Gus O'Connor's brother, Mick, another long-time Boston resident, and many more Clare natives who came out for a great cause and a great night's entertainment.

The next day we went into Boston proper to play a session at Tommy McGann's pub, The Irish Embassy, with Jimmy Noonan, the flute and whistle player, Kitty d'Entremont, his cousin the pianist, and other Boston-based players. After a bit of inner-city driving and trying to find a parking spot (good luck) close by, we made our way to Tommy's. Micho was a bit deflated at first when he realized it wasn't the actual "Irish Embassy at all," that we were heading to. But that mood passed quickly as soon as Tommy, a truly fine gentleman, welcomed his dear countryman (as he did many to America – helped them find a "start") to his establishment in Boston. Micho's fame preceded him at many such engagements, but he was always as down-to-earth and as humble as a Clare farmer could wish to be. And with someone like Tommy, you could sense it was more important to Micho that he was meeting a neighbor and friend – someone from home. Those were his real touchstones throughout his rambles in the world; good friends that he felt he was in good company with, and even better if they enjoyed and appreciated his music. He took playing music for others very seriously, too: "It's a gift, and there's a saying that if you don't share a gift, you'll lose it." This was an intrinsic quality that one who possesses a charitable and sensitive nature, such as Micho, or such as Paddy Shannon, the Fisher Street *Shanachie* and a Parish contemporary of Micho's, arrived at through many long years of belief and the honest effort of trying to live a good and decent life.

We left out of there after a good time was had by all, and a rake of good tunes had been played, and we headed west on the Mass. Pike, hoping to get home to Cottekill (about a 4 hour drive) by sometime around midnight. I had to be the one to say, "let's hit the road," as I knew I had a busy life to get back to, and also because I had made this same journey many times and knew it to be a long and rather dull, straight slog; especially at night. We said our good-byes and thanked Gerry and Tommy for a great visit to "Boshton."

As we faced the old-boat-of-a-Buick westward and drove on out back towards the Hudson Valley, which lay some 30 or 40 miles beyond the far western border of Massachusetts, it gradually began to dawn on us that Micho's time in America was drawing short. This thought was accompanied by a twinge of sadness, naturally, but I also felt a warm sense of accomplishment well up in me, something I also had felt returning from Philly that late night a week before: this had really been a tremendously worthwhile and rewarding experience; what a trip.

After a few days back in Cottekill, we held a nice farewell party for Micho at my house, and many of the friends and neighbors he'd met came to send him off in good form, and a few folks who hadn't been able to meet him before or attend the concert at the College were able to enjoy hearing him in our living room. Pat Flannery came over to partake, and he also let me know, on the quiet, that Micho had asked him to take him down to confession at St. Peter's. He said that he thought Micho probably wanted to "get right with the Man above -- before flying out, just in case, like." Micho was deeply touched by the great fondness and welcome he was given that night and in America in general, and I think he also gained a long over-due sense of true professionalism; he had been paid very well all along the way. I could tell he was also a bit torn about leaving all these new and warm-hearted friends. He'd been away from Doolin for a good long while, though, and we'd only telephoned his brother, Gussie, once during the visit to see how he was and let him know Micho was doing fine and to fill him in on when he'd return, etc., and I could sense Micho was longing for his own home and his dear brother, too.

Micho went to Mass that Sunday morning, the day of his return flight to Shannon, driven down to Rosendale and back by the Flannerys. We had a leisurely late breakfast then, and afterwards, Micho completed packing which never took long for the rambler. I knew he had a money-belt that he'd bought in Germany ("A fast man with a knife could have that from you, too," he'd also mentioned), so I asked him if we should roll up the check I had written, totaling close to $4,000 U.S. dollars, from all the combined and accumulated funds he had earned from all the paying gigs and concerts (less petrol money), and put it in the money-belt for safekeeping for the trip home? I told him to deposit the check in his bank branch in Ennistymon when he got home, and all would be well. Just as we were doing this, Pat Flannery came to the door to say a last goodbye and Micho said: "We'd better get that put into the belt before the Mayo Man gets here." Micho fondly said goodbye to him, Travis and Luke, and also little Stephen. Ellen took our picture in the yard before we headed the blessed old Buick off back southward towards the airport. As we started down the hill on lower Cottekill Road, having travelled only a few country blocks from the house, Micho asked: "Do you suppose I might ever come back to America?"

I said: "Sure, of course you will, Micho," adding: "I can tell you one thing for sure, though, my friend, I'm quite certain you are the only man in America right now that could make that much money with a tin whistle in that short amount of time."

"Is that right?" he responded, adding: "Ah, Faith, that's great." I then asked, while it was still on my mind, if he had any of that money left from the original cash he'd brought over with him, and if so, I explained that I would change it back from dollars into pounds at the airport. "Faith, no . . ., I haven't," he said, "I gave it all to the priest this morning."

So there goes Micho back home to Doolin, having toured all around the Eastern seaboard of America for nearly a month or more, while carrying less than $40.00 dollars cash in his pocket, and at the end of that tour gives what's left of it to our local Parish Priest. There he goes back on the plane carrying only the small canvas bag and a plastic sack, the same way he'd come "into Amerikay," the only difference being that there was a nice pay-check folded up in the money-belt, and he was wearing an American Eagle-Washington, DC emblazoned sweatshirt.

Second Tour and Final Visit:

As previously mentioned, Micho's next tour, about a year-and-a half later, in the middle of a good, hot, NY summer, was mainly organized by Bill Ochs for the making of a documentary video in New York City. Micho would also return to the Mid-Hudson Valley and stay with us again in Cottekill, and also spend a few days with Dennis and Lois Cremmins and their girls, who had recently moved house to a place called Purdys, NY, farther north but still in Westchester County. Dennis also volunteered again for some van driving stints, but for the most part, Micho's time was spent in or around the city, filming the interview sections of the video in the So Ho section of Lower Manhattan, and with Bill Ochs in Mid-town, and staying with various volunteers who had guest-room space for our visiting Irish minstrel; like his cousin, Teresa O'Dea and her husband, Klaus Hein, and with another piper friend and former student of Bill's, Jim Markham, and his family out in Englewood, New Jersey. Jim was a member of the well-known Kearney (NJ) Pipe and Drum Band, and he and his wife and daughter also accompanied Bill and Micho on a Circle Line Ferry cruise around Manhattan. We had a few gigs organized, the main one being the Snug Harbor Festival on Staten Island, which was first up, and the premier event would then be the concert in Greenwich Village Church (which would also be filmed and recorded for the documentary project) at the end of this second tour back in New York City.

The big rave-up in the pop media world that summer was the opening of Spike Lee's *Malcolm X* movie. My son, Stephen, and all of his friends and a great portion of the youth in New York that year were all swept up in the marketing campaign and were sporting *Malcolm X* baseball caps. While buying one for Stevie, he and Dennis Cremmins thought Micho should also have one as a welcome gift. Micho immediately donned the hat, put his Irishman's cap into his bag, and wore the *Malcolm X* baseball cap for the most part of the rest of the tour -- when in Rome . . .? Along with various light-colored tee shirts, sunglasses, and his amulet necklace around his neck (in New Orleans they would call it a "gri-gri"); and with the braces (suspenders) strapped on for gigs and for "stepping up to the plow," and wearing the copper magnetic bracelet (good for the blood pressure)on his wrist; and with a large-buckled leather belt, reefing in "the corporation" (to use Brud Petty's term for the manly girth), and with sandals on his feet for footwear and occasionally a sport coat for the cooler or more formal moments, Micho looked and fit the perfect image of just another Star, ambling about Manhattan in a comfortable disguise.

This is how he appeared as he looked out on the crowds at the Snug Harbor Festival, which was held on the grounds of the old Merchant Mariners Retirement Home, on Staten Island. Little Stephen had a fun day there playing with other kids around the extensive gardens and by the duck ponds on the grounds.

As we pulled up that day in Dennis' van, the first person we met was a man by the name of Paul Keating, one of the festival organizers and volunteers, and another Irish music supporter, journalist and critic. He was thrilled to meet Micho (there had been a great buzz and expectancy about that first appearance at this festival: the premier NY Irish Folk Festival at the time), and again, he also kind of looked at Dennis and me with that: "Who in hell's blue blazes . . . How did they . . .?" gaze. Paul and I eventually did have a good talk before that day was out, and agreed that Bill would bring Micho up to him in East Durham, in Greene County, up in the Catskills, for a NY Clare Association gathering at one of the resort/bungalow colonies up there, later on towards the end of the tour, and I would come up and collect him afterwards. Keating has been a major mover and shaker in the traditional Irish music world in New York and has lately been the Artistic Director (for the past few years) of The Catskill Irish Arts Week, held each summer up there in East Durham. It's a pity Micho didn't live long enough to see or be a part of one of those ensuing festivals: He would have loved to see the growth and developing enthusiasm for the evolving traditional music scene that is so apparent up there every summer.

Micho played an afternoon set at Snug Harbor on that fine sunny day – a flute and whistle, workshop-like, themed presentation -- and then performed as a headliner on the evening main-stage, on what was a beautiful, mild, starlit mid-summer's night. There were great performances that night by younger players such as Liz Carroll and Daithi Sproule, Joanie Madden and Cherish the Ladies, and also Johnny Cunningham definitely blew all of us away with his fiery, impassioned fiddling. Then a group of senior, NY veterans of the NY Traditional Irish Music world came on: Andy McGann, Jack Coen, and Felix Dolan. It was a real treat to see these gents perform, especially to someone like me who for the most part had only heard of them, never actually meeting or seeing them play live. Mick Moloney was the M.C. for the main stage and had given them a proper introduction, and the sound system was impeccable. Seated, mostly on blankets or folding chairs, out on the hillside lawn facing the stage, under the evening stars, we could all hear our own "stars" beautifully.

Micho and I were standing out on the field to stage-left, amongst the audience listening to these well-known, successful practitioners of Traditional Irish Music, and I was keeping an eye on Mick Moloney, as he'd said he would signal me when Micho should make his way up the steps to the stage, at stage-right. I assumed we would circle around the back of the crowd and make our way up there, and I was getting a bit anxious to do so, but when the time came and Mick began introducing MIcho at the stand-up microphone, doesn't Micho saunter off right across in front of the stage and the entire audience, with his flute and whistle in his hands, held behind his back as he was wont to do, leaning forward (towards the plow?), wearing a white shirt, sandals, and with the braces on, and on up to that mic, just as Mick finished his introduction. There was a brief hesitation for a moment, as a young lady stage-hand came over, and, leaning up towards Micho seemed to be whispering in his ear and pointing, alerting him to the fact that they had already set him up for a sit-down mic and chair at center stage. What we heard next over the PA system was: "Sure, I'll give it a 'blasht' right here!" And as he stood there and the music came out of his big-timber flute, I can tell you, it was truly astonishing. A sense of Pan-like charm, mystery and delight enthralled us all. It was a purely magical moment, and I couldn't have been happier for Micho, or more proud of him than on that evening, indeed . . . It was also heart-lifting to see him so well received by the main New York audience for his type of music, and then backstage to hear Jack Coen say: "Micho, you always were the best, and you still are."

With that great success behind him on this second tour, and with a renewed sense of confidence quite apparent in his demeanor, Micho buckled down and did step up to the plow (a phrase he'd become very fond of using by now), and diligently went to work with Bill on making the video. Mick Moloney is also the featured interviewer on this tape (and also M.C. of the Greenwich Village Church concert that was coming up) and most of the question/answer sessions were filmed and recorded in a professional studio way down near lower Broadway on Broome Street, in the So Ho section of lower Manhattan. Some of those segments were filmed outside in the open air of a small, brick-walled backyard there at Global Village Productions.

The weather was at times purely stifling (I thought); hot and humid, way downtown on the street there, and it had that real, NY, summer-in-the-city feel to it. This was true even up in the shady, tree-lined streets on the sidewalks of Greenwich Village where we were also shuttling to and fro for rehearsals and eventually for the concert. It would also be lovely up there some evenings, though, when a small breeze would find its way down the streets, and reach us as we walked along the blocks not far from Washington Square Park. I thought the heat might get to "Big Mike" (another pet name that some folks close to him also used) at some point that summer, but he did unexpectedly well with it, and I never heard a complaint. Many of my Irish friends have told me how unbearable they found the heat and hot sun of New York in summer to be. "It'd 'roasht' ye," as Gussie Russell would say of even a temperately hot day back in Clare in summer.

At this point in Micho's life, though (nearing 80 years of age), he appeared to me to be in the best of health during these days (some of his last in America as it turns out) – looking and feeling much healthier than he had in many years. This much-improved sate of health was greatly helped by dietary advice and mild, oral blood-sugar control medicines which had been prescribed by his Doctor back home in Ireland: a woman he had enormous respect for (and whom he listened to). Also, the years of eye-drop therapy for his tear-duct and sore-eye condition had finally relieved much of what had been nearly constant irritation for a long time. He was in great form in terms of his playing as well, and he was immensely pleased with his performance at the Greenwich Village Church concert and filming.

Not one to boast at all, Micho did however intimate to me that night backstage after the concert that he was very happy he'd been able to, "play for that long of a job and not make any bad notes, you see." That concert and the resultant video and CD, to me, represented a kind of crowning achievement in his career at that point in time, as was certainly true for these New York tours in the early 1990's: a real professional high water mark, if you will, for this humble, dear sweet man, Micho Russell, the musicianer with the farmer's ways about him, from up in Luogh, in Doolin, Co. Clare, Ireland. The same man who could receive a post card up there on that remote hillside, on the rural, far western coast of Clare, which had been sent to him from a fan living in Germany and addressed simply to: "Micho, Ireland."

Mick Moloney's introduction for the concert that night was both entertaining and succinct and it gave Micho a great nod of respect and appreciation. It included a humorous anecdote about Micho's first visit to England, and how they were eventually able to find out Micho's sister's address in Shepherds Bush where he was to stay, which, naturally, he hadn't remembered to bring with him. Micho, in his often comical state of innocence, simply imagined he'd find a small village with a large bush growing in the central square (somewhere near London!), and that by asking around, surely he would find someone who knew where she lived. The whole story is transcribed and included in the booklet that accompanies the CD, *The Whistling Ambassador*, but I can say it involves somehow getting in touch with his brother, Gussie, back in Doolin, via the Post Mistress's telephone, timed perfectly for a return-home bicycle journey , on a Sunday just after Mass. Many events like this, in the lives of the Russells (and others in Clare, like the Kilhourhys, John and Paddy, for instance, also known as the "Tarberts") were truly folklore in the making, gaining longevity as they are told and re-told along the way.

During one of the interview segments on the video, and there are many interesting question-and-answer exchanges on it that are worth the price of admission alone, one in particular stands out in my mind: that is when Moloney asked him about the learning and playing of the music when he was a young boy and in his teenage years, and: "What did the music mean to him back then?" Micho didn't hesitate a moment: "It meant everything," he said. I've also heard Micho tell of seeing his first glimpse of a man playing a tin whistle at a house party when he was a boy, and that what struck him about the experience along with the actual sound was how the man's fingers looked to be "artistic" to him.

I've mentioned earlier how Micho felt that having the music in his life in his later years was a great balm to him, and I would say it was obvious to me in those days what he meant. He kept going with it, and as age began to come on him, the music began to return and repay the loyalty; it opened new doors for him continually. Before he'd hardly left to return home that year there was already talk of booking him in the future at the Wolf Trap Heritage Folk Festival in Washington DC, and maybe a trip out to San

Francisco. And Bill Ochs did actually have him return once more that next year, for a third and final visit to specifically record additional music for *The Whistling Ambassador* CD, and some additional archival and field recording material as well.

If there was any one thing I could single out as an important gift that Micho gave me concerning this personal involvement with the music, it was the understanding of how important and fulfilling it is to enjoy your own music and your personal engagement with the process of learning and playing it -- "having a tune for yourself," as he would say, as he would similarly say of "having a prayer." Not simply saying one, or playing one, but to have one -- to possess it in ones being. There are plenty of reasons people take up an instrument or begin to learn songs to sing, but at the heart of the best of it is a craving for it, an inner need to pursue it, a drive in one to master a part of it that speaks to your heart. It's first and foremost a "heart thing," in my mind, and Micho had a great way of reminding one of that. If you are lucky enough to have a gift for it, then you'll also, hopefully, find a way to share it. My life has been enormously blessed by having met and become a friend of Micho Russell's, and that's something you can definitely take to the bank.

Micho came back for that final visit a year later (fall of 1993), as I've said, mostly to record a CD and some archival material for Bill Ochs. Picking him up at the airport that time, I had another surprise as I waited for him to appear at the International Arrivals gate. I waited 'till the end again, and then out he comes rolling in a wheelchair, being pushed along by another Aer Lingus attendant. My first thought was, naturally, that he had injured himself somehow, but up he stands to meet me, grinning, and saying: "I copped on to this in Germany last year – It's very handy." I guess it was one of the benefits of the aging process – accepting a lift when it's offered – not something he was entirely unfamiliar with, for sure.

Back up in Cottekill for the last few days of that final (as it turned out) visit, Micho recorded some tunes and songs for Bill Ochs in my living room. Bill had come up from the city with a big bag full of good recording equipment and gear to do the job with, and those recordings they made there, and in New York would either make it onto the CD, or might just be used for archival purposes. That room had pretty good acoustics and a nice hardwood floor, and on a few of those takes you can hear Micho's alternating and syncopated feet tapping away, and even Stephen's dog, Bebop, barking in the background. My favorite cut from those sessions which did make its way onto the CD is, "The Steam Roller MacTeigue's Polka," and its insightful, reminiscent introduction. Many of his introductory prefaces are absolutely great sources of pure folklore in themselves, any one of which could be a jumping-off spot for those interested in folklore as an academic pursuit, or as starting places to begin piecing together an understanding of traditional themes and specifically Irish cultural themes. He also recorded some pieces during that session that he rarely played out in public, and a few he had not played in many, many years, and certainly had never recorded before.

Once again the time for leaving and heading home arrived, and after farewells were said, and Micho and I sat back into the motorcar – the big yellow Buick -- and headed off for our drive down the hill and on southward down the Hudson Valley towards the airport, in almost the same spot as before, a few blocks from the house, where he'd asked about ever returning to America, this time instead of a questioning tone, though, he announced quite boldly and confidently: "You never know, I might be shoving back into America next year. I've become terribly fond of New York." If only that could have been so, we had no idea then that that would be the last time we would ever travel together.

Late that following winter of 1994, towards the end of February and only a couple weeks before I was due to fly back over to Ireland when we would hopefully take up some new adventures together, I received a call in the late-night, early-morning hours, which I answered out in my converted garden-shed-office in Cottekill, as I was up late writing. It was from Ronan Quinlan in Dublin. He was a staff photographer at the time for the Irish Press, a daily Dublin newspaper, and had seen the report as soon as it came in that Micho had died in a car crash on the Galway Road at Kilcolgan.

Apparently a risky u-turn had been made and an on-coming car, most likely travelling too fast as well, had crested and come over the hill, colliding straight-on into the passenger side of the vehicle Micho was riding in. He had been still alive as he was taken by ambulance to the hospital in Galway, and the shocking news had come down to the village in Doolin in time for Susan O'Connor to drive Gussie to Galway; she recalls Gussie hoping Micho had only taken "a bad knock." Unfortunately he died of his internal injuries in the emergency room, and then the real shock began to sink in when word made it back to Doolin, and to all the friends in Fisher Street , so many of whom were like family – who **were** family for all intents and purposes.

A huge hole had been rent into the soul and fabric of the entire community that night, as grief fell upon his native village and home; where he had always been the one big star and friend everyone could count on to lift their spirits; and where he had always been such a pre-eminent, iconic figure who ennobled their rural, traditional agrarian world. Their famous folk musician and their hugely lovable, local friend and character had passed on due to a tragic accident. It was both too hard to take or comprehend, and yet it also immediately seemed like an unwanted inevitability that one had to accept: to swallow like an extremely bitter medicine; it was a threshold you had to cross. It was like some kind of divine, indelible stamp being placed on an already growing mythological stature and reputation; a destiny that takes some stars and some great people to an even higher place by force of the untimely, the unexpected, and the seemingly unwarranted tragedy. Micho used to quote the blind poet, Ó Raferty, in his introduction to one of the few slow airs he played: "When it comes to the tragedy, Man's hope is vain." The sadness incurred by Micho Russell's untimely accidental death had that bitter sense of loss that nothing but time can assuage. It fell on Ireland far and wide that February, as well.

I managed, somehow, against many odds, in firstly getting a grievance allowance for a change of ticket and schedule from my originally booked trip, and in getting on the next available flight from JFK, and I just made it to the funeral, having also caught a lift from my dear friend (and one of Micho's, too), Cyril O'Donoghue, the phenomenal contemporary folksinger, guitarist and Irish bozouki player, who picked me up and drove us from Shannon out to the Doolin Church just in time for the Mass.

The grief-stricken look on poor GussieRussell's face that day spoke for us all. A beautiful Mass and Eulogy was said for Micho by Father John O'Donohue; and the Carrick-on-Suir poet, Michael Coady, read as a concelebrant and urged us to always: "Remember the living man." A huge honor was also bestowed on Micho that day, as Mary Robinson, the President of Ireland, had a military Colonel represent her there at the funeral. Tears come to my eyes every time I mention that touching recognition, even to this day some 15 years later. This was something that had never occurred before in honor of a Clare farmer. It was such a fitting and touching testament to Micho's goodness, and a high tribute to his unrelenting personal love for his country -- his beloved Ireland.

The weather couldn't have been worse that day as we followed behind Gussie and the casket from the church, across the road and down into the graveyard where the burial words and prayers were said and tunes were played. It was as if nature, too, was raging against this unfortunate human event. With lashing rain and gale-like winds driving it into our faces we wept and prayed and railed against the black day -- the end of an era -- the loss of our most tangible and recognizable link to the traditional past. I recall the outpouring of grief by so many that day: Tony McMahon was totally heart-broken; and Micho's sister, Bridie, was beside herself with grief; sadness was also apparent in other family members who had come from distant homes in Ireland and England, and on the faces of so many friends from the community, too many to list here. Lastly, though, I recall Eugene Lambe, sitting on his upturned instrument case, with the cold pouring rain dripping down his head and face, playing a slow air on his big full-set of Uilleann Pipes – rain be damned -- and then looking up to me as I stood nearby, and saying: "Poor Big Mike."

Micho's death was not only a national news-story, the funeral having been covered by RTE Television and Radio, but also an international one as well, reaching even as far as the New York Irish newspapers and the Irish Times obituary column. Of course, many local newspaper and radio programs around Clare devoted numerous articles and essays and interviews to the event, and one of my favorite comments came, again, from Eugene Lambe, the piper and instrument maker, and a long time friend of Micho's. His insightful, non-maudlin, and beautifully succinct quote concerning Micho's passing was: "He always loved automobiles, and he had a great fondness for women, and he was with the both of them at the end."

Almost everyone I spoke to also felt deeply sorry for, and expressed sincere condolences towards the poor American woman who had been driving when the accident occurred. She'd been doing just what I had done so many times and had planned to do again shortly that spring; and what many hundreds of others had done so often: drive Micho around Ireland -- to or from home; or, to and from house parties; or home up the steep winding road that leads up Doonagore, returning from late night sessions around Clare; or into Ennis, or to and from the airports; or, for that matter, all around the streets and highways of a foreign country, as well. As I said in a speech given at the second memorial weekend in February, 1996: "This accident could easily have happened to any of us. Dying in a road accident was a high risk probability and a distinct occupational hazard for the travelling musician." And if Micho Russell was anything, he was definitely a travelling musician.

I recall driving home from a long day and night spent down in Joe McHugh's Pub in Liscannor, and Micho and I had been in the company of Tom Murphy, an Aer Lingus pilot who also came down to Doolin from his home in Dublin, to unwind, recharge the old batteries and rest the frayed nerves which were the inevitable result of high pressured life in the big outside world of commerce and air travel. Relaxing with the likes of Micho and Gussie, and Paddy and John Kilourhy in the musical houses of those wonderful publicans like McHugh and the Oconnors, and absorbing the good music and times "down west" definitely had a refreshing and somehow inspiring effect on us. Tom had enormous respect and time for the old fellows and the characters, and like myself, simply enjoyed hanging out with them. From the rear passenger seat, as we headed up the dark, winding hill through Moher and St.Bridgit's Well, Tom said: "You have a lovely slow way of driving, Dennis. It's greatly appreciated back here." How ironic it is for me to think of this now, and yet we all took our chances on the highways back then, you had to if you were going to get around the countryside to wherever the music was going on.

Over the course of my friendship with Micho, which lasted over a decade, I had become close enough to him to ask, at one point, as intimate a question as this: "If you had your life to live over, Micho, what would you have done differently?" I was almost certain his answer would be something along the lines of having managed to have married and settled into a more domestic, farmer and householder oriented life. But the unexpected response he gave was: "I wish I'd been a better businessman, so I could drive my own car."

The enormous amount of irony lodged in this remark becomes truly bittersweet when we look back on the way he died. I felt It was additionally ironic and poignant in that, as I explained earlier, he was finally coming into the full of his health for the first time in a long while. But there we are, "that's the way, now," and still, we can take his philosophical advice to heart and, "just, keep going . . . ."

Down on Fisher Street two years later, after the evening I'd given my speech at the memorial concert, which was still held in the church then – today it is held annually in The Russell Center, a fitting name for the active community center; with its concert hall, classrooms, and football pitch out behind – and after Gus O'Connor and I were also interviewed later that night in Gus's living room by the Irish Community Radio, Raidió na Gaeltachta, reporters who were in from Connemara covering the event, I heard several follow-up details and opinions concerning Micho's accident and his last ramble.

Bridie O'Brien, who like many locals had known Micho all her life, said she'd met Micho in the street there outside the door of the Pub in Fisher Street the day before he headed off to the party in Spiddal, and said she thought he looked fit and was in fine fettle and great form; and they'd had a laugh together, she told me, over her asking: "So, how are the women treatin' you, Micho?" and he had replied: "I think the divils are only coddin' me, Blasht it . . . ."

Another Fisher Street native, a man not too much younger than Micho, but maybe a generation behind, said he thought that what it was that finally "caught Micho out," he felt, "was that Micho was getting forgetful. He'd forgotten his oul' jacket back out at that party he'd played for out in Spiddal, in Connemara. When he remembered it, he asked that American woman to turn around all of a sudden, like, and to stop in at a Petrol Station there on the main road at the cross by Kilcolgan, so he could go telephonin' back to the house they'd left from and tell them out there to keep an eye out for the oul' jacket. An' to tell you the truth, it was something he could have just as easily thrown out and bought himself another one like it for short money in town. I think it's forgetfulness that caught him out. I do. But she, being a Yank, probably wasn't great at them u-turns either, you see. And you can bet the ones that were comin' over the hill were probably flyin' it, too, and bang! Micho got the bad knock on his side of the car. A pure pity, it was . . ."

I stopped in for a quiet drink later one evening as that weekend in '96 drew to a close, up at the far north end of town towards Ballyreen (where Brud Petty lived), at Mrs. Linnane's, Atlantic View. She was the only one about the place and came out to tend the bar in the guest lounge there, and with a dusky evening sun setting off behind *Inis Oir*, and the soft evening light coming through the west window we chatted about Micho's passing.

She heard it was his spleen that had been badly damaged and that he died of internal bleeding, and ultimately, heart failure. Like many, we commiserated and lamented the fact that it was extremely sad that Micho, such a gentle soul, should have to die in such a violent manner. It was just truly a pity, we agreed. Then she told me that she thought that the injury was especially ironic from her point of view because she remembered Micho having had an accident coming down a steep hill, driving the horse and side-car back home from Ennistymon, long ago when he was a young man, and she believed he had also suffered severe injury to his spleen and organs on that same side of his body way back then.

I'd never heard this story before, and there is much about Micho I certainly never knew, or would ever be able to know. As an outsider, one who doesn't even hardly qualify as a "blow-in" (a non-native who moves in to live in the Parish), and as only one of many who befriended him primarily through the music and who happened to spend a lot of time with the man, I can only say, like all human stories, his is also larger and far more complex and more deeply private than any one of us outside that life will ever know.

Part of the great beauty of this life, and its inhabitants, for me, is that there is, in fact, just so very much of the unknown about it: so much to ponder on; and to "study-up on-the-quiet" about; so many tunes and stories to listen to, to learn; to learn about and from; so many rambles to take; and so many incredible people to discover.

In the heel of the hunt, then, as this reminiscence comes to a close, I would only like to add that although I have tried to present Micho in as honest a fashion as I possibly could, perhaps at times that presentation has seemed to the reader to be too preoccupied with presenting only the up-side of things, with the seemingly fantastic, and with the purely successful elements of my story (save for the funeral, of course) dominating the narrative. I do not want the reader to mistakenly think that all of my time and travels with Micho were simply some kind of idyllic trundle down an Irish path, through the charming rose-garden gate, and on over across the emerald fields and braes, and along the quaint by-ways of the lovely and charming, old sod; or, that this memoir is meant to cross over, even minutely, into the realm of American-born, or emigrant nostalgia; or the sentimental, fairytale-like yarns that get spun from those imaginative skeins. That would be a huge disservice to the reality of this story and the real human qualities of the main characters, Micho and Gussie Russell, and the very real interactions we had as friends – as real people. Pakie had died and was already a major mythological figure by the time I ventured down to Doolin.

Truth be told, MIcho and I had several rows over the years; crossed wires, missed communications, and Gussie and I did, too. In fact, when you've been sternly sent down the road by Gussie, you won't forget it, I can tell you! Micho could rear-up on you, as well, and often it was due to the result of my having fallen in with the wrong company, or by somehow involving a questionable third party; or some events just happened which caused an old grudge to surface, something that may have actually had very little to do with me; but due to loose-talk, or simply by being unaware of sensitive histories, I found myself in Micho's dog-house on at least several, memorable occasions.

These rough patches were always gotten through, thankfully, and perhaps some of those touchier experiences taught me more about life, and in particular, Irish ways, than the whimsical ones ever possibly could. Sometimes it took only a day or two for the ruffled feathers to settle, sometimes a little longer, but forgiveness among friends is a great thing and tends to strengthen relationships immeasurably. It was certainly always a great relief to me when I found myself back in the good graces of either of the Russell brothers.

Throughout Micho's visits with us in America, there were also plenty of instances when many other folks hoped they could commandeer him away from us for a night or two: "to an oul' party," or off to play at someone's favorite local session, far from our beaten path, and the like. And certainly, neither Bill Ochs nor I would have ever stood in the way of Micho doing something he really wanted to do, but he had a way of steering clear of uncertain situations, an inner radar and instinct, which he summed up to Bill one night out in the urban, social wilds of Philadelphia this way: "Some of those people are the kind who are only out for a bit of sport, and you wouldn't know where they might land you." Kitty d'Entrement perhaps put it best: "Micho was wise – he truly had a wisdom."

At the close of his summer visit in 1992, after his ferry cruise on the Circle Line, Bill had also taken him for a double-decker bus tour around Manhattan, and as Micho and he sat up topside and passed by Saint Patrick's Cathedral on Fifth Avenue, Micho exclaimed : "There's a lot of folks in Clare 'would love to see this!" And shortly before leaving New York, Bill asked once more if there was anything else he might like to do? He replied: "Faith, no -- I think I have the lot of it seen."

Long before the Russell Brothers were ever born, their father, Austin Rua Russell, returned home to his wife, Annie (nee Moloney), at their farm-house in Luogh, from a fair he'd been to in Miltown Malbay, sometime in the first decade of the 20th Century. He revealed to her that there had been Gypsies (Roms) at the fair, and that he had paid them a fee and had his fortune told. They had prophesied that three sons would be born to them, and that those sons would become famous. Micho only told me this when he was in his mid- to late 60s, but from that place in time it seemed to have been an uncanny prediction. The Russells, of course, were never ones to value fame, and I seriously doubt they ever thought of themselves as such. But it's all tied up in the folklore, you see, and, "Aye, there's the rub . . ." you might not always be able to tell where history and lore intersect and merge; somewhere out along the road, where truth and myth wrestle for supremacy. To "Just, keep going . . . ," now, that's the way, now . . . .

Notes:

Pg. 2 -- Winter, D.C. *Those Days in Doolin: My Times with the Tradition-makers* -- projected publication of this ethnographic memoir, which covers the Doolin scene from 1983 on into the first decade of the new millennium, is slated for fall, 2012.

Pg. 13 -- Coady, Michael, *The Well of Spring Water: A Memoir of Micho and Pakie Rusell*. (Carrick-on-Suir, Ireland: 1996). This is by far the best place to start reading about the Russells of Doolin, and to my knowledge the only in-depth, written study of Pakie.

Pg.15 – Dennis Cremmins, (1952 -- 2000), a dear friend and devoted father, husband and musician, passed away, sadly and prematurely due to an in-operable form of cancer (R.I.P.)

Pg. 23 -- Bill Ochs commented in a reflection piece he wrote called, "First Contacts with Micho", commenting on that first gig at the Eagle Tavern: "When it was all over we went smiling into the cold New York night. I was even more deeply moved by Micho than I had been in 1974 (our first meeting in Ireland). His spirit was utterly contagious. Though I had been in a musical doldrums for a year or so, when the concert was over and the last goodbyes had been said, I took out my tin whistle and walked two miles home at one o'clock in the morning, playing all the way up Eighth Avenue." (Penny Whistlers Press: NY, NY).

Pg. 55 -- My speech at the second Memorial Weekend was the progenitor of this longer memoir and was entitled: "Rambles with Micho in America." An edited version appears here as Appendix # 3.

Acknowledgements

Many thanks to the following: Myron Bretholz for his careful proofing and critical recommendations concerning the text; and to Bill Ochs for his textual input, generous loans of photos and tune transcriptons, and critical suggestions, and additionally for his enormous support and friendship of Micho; to Dr. Eugene Lambe, and Dr. Mick Maloney for their recognition and good spirited acknowledgement of Micho's special place in the realm of traditional Irish music; and to Dr. Gearóid Ó hAllmhuráin for constant mentoring and encouragement concerning this and my many other folk-lore projects, and for his acute editorial help, as well; special thanks to Michael Coady, Seamus McGrath and Michael Geaney for initially welcoming and guiding me along with them into the realm of Doolin and its many characters and its vast treasure of music and lore; and to the entire O'Connor family for their unfailing welcome and support and for the enduring and often unknown amounts of support they gave to the Russell Brothers throughout the course of their lives (including the cooked Christmas dinner brought up every year!); Warmest regards and thanks to Pete and Toshi Seeger; to the Clancys of Carrick-on-Suir; to the Dunleavys of Doolin and Winchester, MA; and to two extremely important figures in the world of traditional Irish music and arts: Brendan Flynn of Clifden, and Muris ÓRócháin of Milltown Malbay who have both generously applauded and supported the artistic and cultural contributions made by Micho. Thanks finally to family: Ford and Neva Winter of Rye, NY; Stephen Winter of Kingston, NY; Travis Winter of Ithaca, NY; my step-son, Luke Davis; my sister, Gail (Winter) Buschen, for help in so many ways; and to my friends: Eugene Flanagan, the carpenter of Lisdoonvarna; Cyril O'Donoghue and family, of Shannon Town; and Melissa Heckler, who helped keep the wheels rolling; to Jared at Catskill Art & Office Supply; also to Tim Shannon and John Griffin, the Fisher St. fishermen; and finally, sincerest of thanks to Michele and Hartley "Bob" Barclay.

The Photos: A Scrapbook Photo-Essay

All photos by DennisC. Winter (excepting those noted otherwise).

D.C. Winter and Micho Russell – Cottekill, NY

Fisher Street, Doolin – circa 1983 (Note the common garden plots still visible above the buildings on Fisher Street).

Micho and Gussie Russell – O'Connor's Pub

First of many Irish hire-cars: the little blue Fiat.

Ennystymon – well before the Celtic Tiger came to town.

The castle hill road -- heading down from Doonagore.

The lower road, or "old Board of Works road," as it passes on down across the Russell farm land.

The original Russell home – with relic of the Flanagan house to right.

The Moloney house – birthplace of Micho's mother, Annie, and his aunt, Kate, who was renowned locally as a fine concertina player. Their father was called "the Captain," by the family.

Micho holding court -- Dave Wren looking on; listening to the tune with his usual, rapt and steadfast attention.

The best seat in the house: Mary Shannon between "the brothers."

Morning practice in the kitchen – Doonagore house.

Phone call from Chicago at Roy Roger's home in Media, Pa.

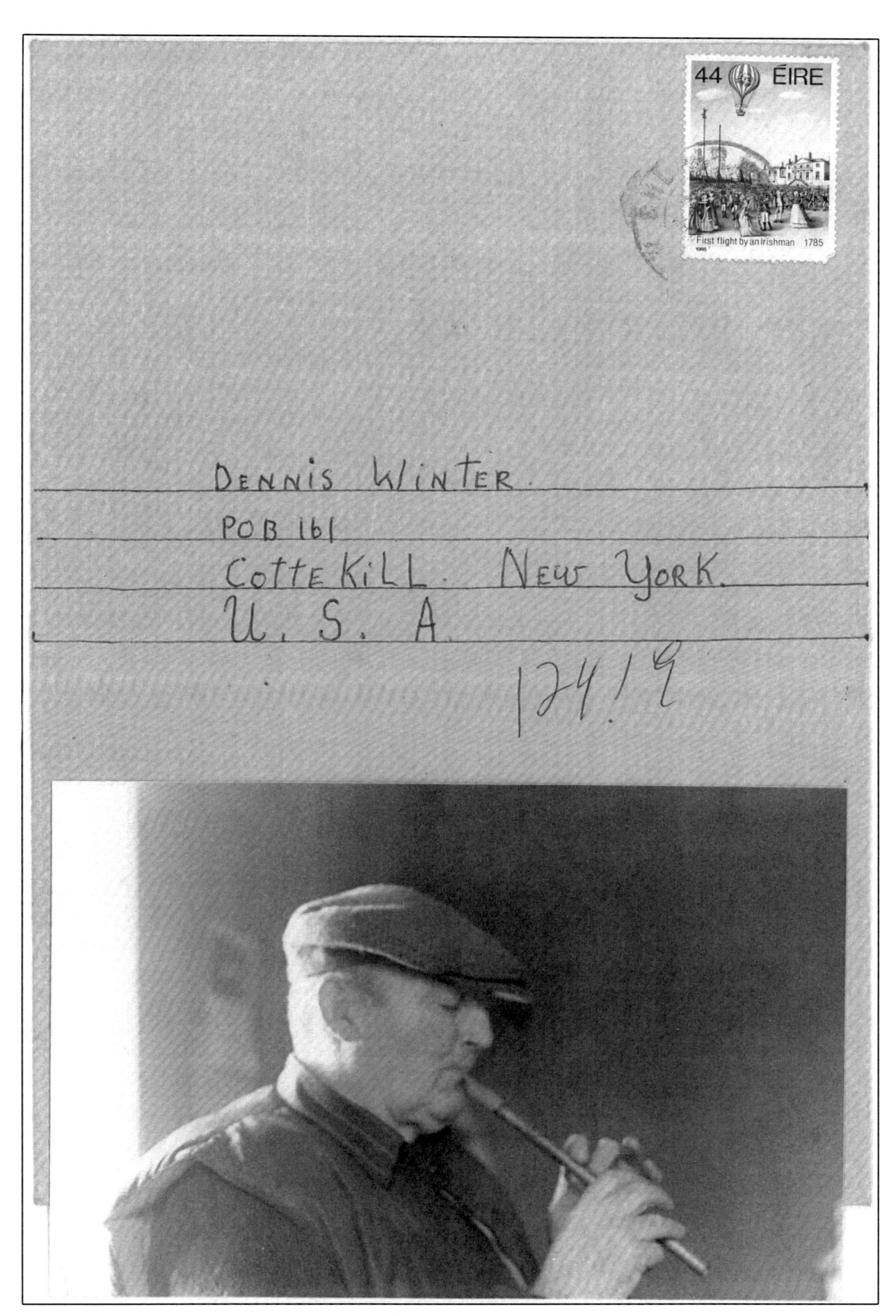

A letter from Micho – text on following pages.

Micho Russell
Doonagore
Doolin
Co Clare
Ireland.
20 — 5 —1985.

Hello Dennis.   I am
Hope You are Well. after Coming home from Scotland had a great Tour. Thanks for the Letter and the Cuttings of the Papour. You asked me for the Air of the Barber Shop You May hear of a Song Called The Limerick Rake or an Old Gaelic Song Called Fágsmide Suid Map ahá Sé. That means we will leave things as they are. But You will have to sing it very Long and slow.

    Key of C   (C TIN Whistle

A ¦ D˙D˙D   C˙I˙D   C B A G   A˙¸
It was in this town Not far from this spot
D E F G   A C A   G˙G   F˙   D˙¸   C˙ NATURAL
That a barber once opened his snyg little shop

D. .D.D   F E D   G A B   C.
he was so Well Tepered his Mind was so pleased
It was said he could coax people in off
   the Street
A .D.D   C A   G. F.   D. .D
It may not Rayme so good   but you
will try and fit it in
    Long   D.
    Short .D
Gussie Told me to those few Word My
Mother God Rest Her sang this Song.

As I Was Coming home from the Fair
   Cappamore
I stepped in light my pipe as any Man Might
   do
Tis there I spied a Colleen With Irish Eyes
   of Blue
And tis then I felt my heart growing quare

   TURN

Chorus
Still I like to Wander down the Old
            Bohepeen
Where the HaweThorn Blossem's are in
            Bloom.
And to sid by the shade in that Old
            Mossy Dale
And to Whisper into Kate Muldoon.

⫟   Key of D
F, E D D,   B A B D   F E D E F D,,
DEFG   BG   F.A.A   F E, D E F E———
DEFG   BG   F A A   F E FED B.,
ABC
D D B A,, B D   F E D   E F   D.,
This is as good as I can do
I have No more Verses   You must Allow
for the beatheng between the Notes

With Eugene Lambe – O'Connor's Pub.

"Big Mike"

Playing the big B-flat whistle -- at Egene Lambe's workshop in Fanore -- late 1980s.

With Hartley "Bob" Barclay – kitchen, Doonagore house, circa 1993.

SING OUT!
THE FOLK SONG MAGAZINE

VOLUME 28/Number 3/1980 — $2.00

Pete Seeger Interview
30th Anniversary Survey
"Encouragement"
"Maple Syrup Time"
"Eight Hour Day"
"Mother's Day Song
Children's Song

30th Anniversary Issue

Micho and I visited Pete Seeger, and he sent us the following two letters.

Dear Dennis — only today
I read your note of last
August — have been swamped.
 Congrats on bringing Micho
to the USA!!! I hope you'll
send info to Sing Out.
   Box 5253
P.S. phone us when   Bethlehem
you get here.   PA 18015
    best Pete

A letter from Pete Seeger.

Another post from Pete Seeger: the song he gave to Micho.

Afternoon performace: Snug Harbor Irish Festival.

The day to head home – Cottekill driveway.

With Pat Flannery and Stevie Winter – Cottekill dining room.

Micho leaning on "Dottie's '72 Buick," with my son, Stephen, in Cottekill, NY.

Travis Ford Winter and Micho Russell – Cottekill living room.

Reading up on the quiet – living room, Cottekill.

With Ellen Winter – Cottekill dining room.

With Travis and Stevie,

and the American Football.

Micho in front of the small garage I had recently built. Not the best photo of Micho, but the Ford Van with the "blue oval" insignia, the American basketball hoop, and Stephen's first cool bike certainly sets the sense of place.

With American football and the author.

Clifden Harbor – Co. Galway

On the way through Connemarra.

Top to bottom: Submarine Service insignia; J.P. Holland's cottage in Liscannor (photo:M. Heckler); the USS James K. Polk, SSBN 645 — the boat I served on in the late 1960's.

With Bill Ochs on the Hudson River Circle Line cruise, (Photo: Ochs Collection).

With Dennis Cremmins – Irvington, NY.

Boarding the Circle Line: with Jim Markham and family; Bill Ochs; and Micho looking quite the Star incognito. (Ochs Collection)

Beside the "Fenian Ram," at the John Phillip Holland exhibit — Patterson, NJ. (Ochs Collection)

General Dynamics Shipbuilding Plant, Groton Conn. Viewed from New London, Conn. Bridge.

Originally the Electric Torpedo Boat Co. (founded and lost to scoundrels by Holland), then referred to as simply Electric Boat, now the General Dynamics Shipyard where many submarines (including the Polk), have been built, and where my father worked on the Nautilus. View from New London, Conn. Pier on the Thames River -- 2009.

William E. Winter, Machinst's Mate 1st Class – circa 1943.

My mother and father, Dorothy and Bill Winter – Hawthorne, NY, circa 1943.

Hard-hat Salvage Diver's Diploma.

Seaman Apprentic, D Winter, heading off to Sub. School Hawthorne, NY, 1966

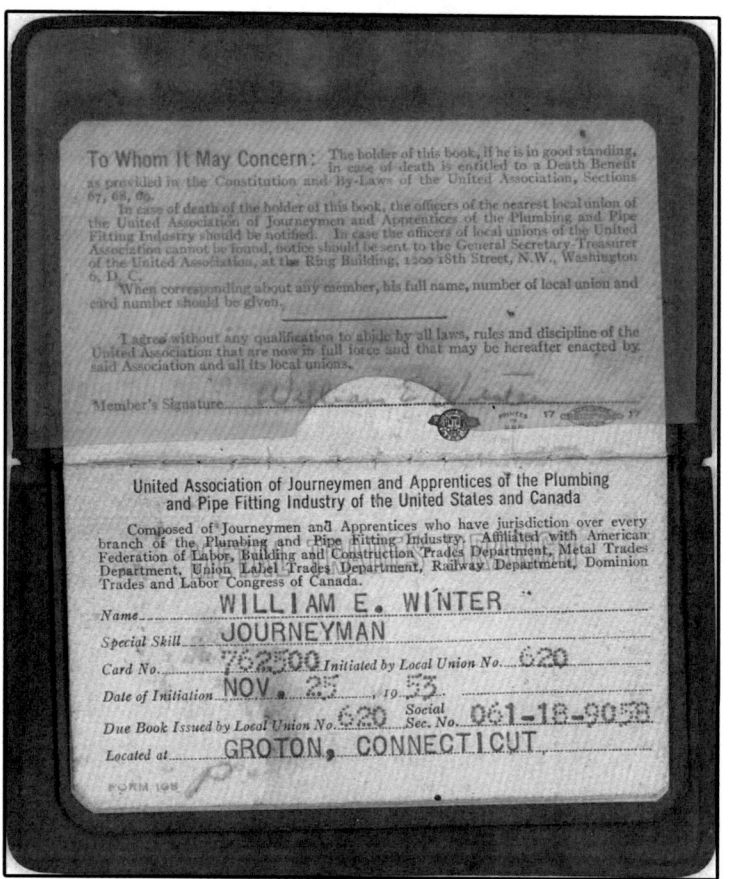

Plumbing and Pipe Fitters Union Card: My father, Bill Winter, worked on the Nautilus at Electric Boat, Groton, Conn., In the late 1950s. He often used to tell of how he had to work late into the night, on into the graveyard shift, in order to finish silver-soldering the fittings and valves for the ship's whistle, so that it could be sounded next day as it slid down the ways into the Thames River, after Mamie Eisenhower, the First Lady, had swung the Champagne bottle and Christened the boat; the first nuclear powered submarine, and the first boat to navigate across beneath Polar ice-cap.

This posed photo was originally taken for use as the cover for *Doolin's Micho Russell:A Portrait*. c. 1990.

With Michael Geaney -- Fisher Street, circa 1985.

Dennis Cremmins and Micho -- Greenwich Village, NYC.

The life-long discipline.

With Tommy McGann – at Tommy's, Irish Embassy Pub, Boston Ma

Tunes at the Woodstock Pub -- 1991.

With Jimmy Scales, owner of the Woodstock Pub, Ulster Co. NY.

Interview with a *Woodstock Times*, newspaper reporter.

Bill Ochs and Micho Russell – tunes at Gus Hayes' Tara Rest. Yonkers, NY

Session at McGann's Irish Embassy Pub, with Kitty d'Entremont and Jim Noonan.

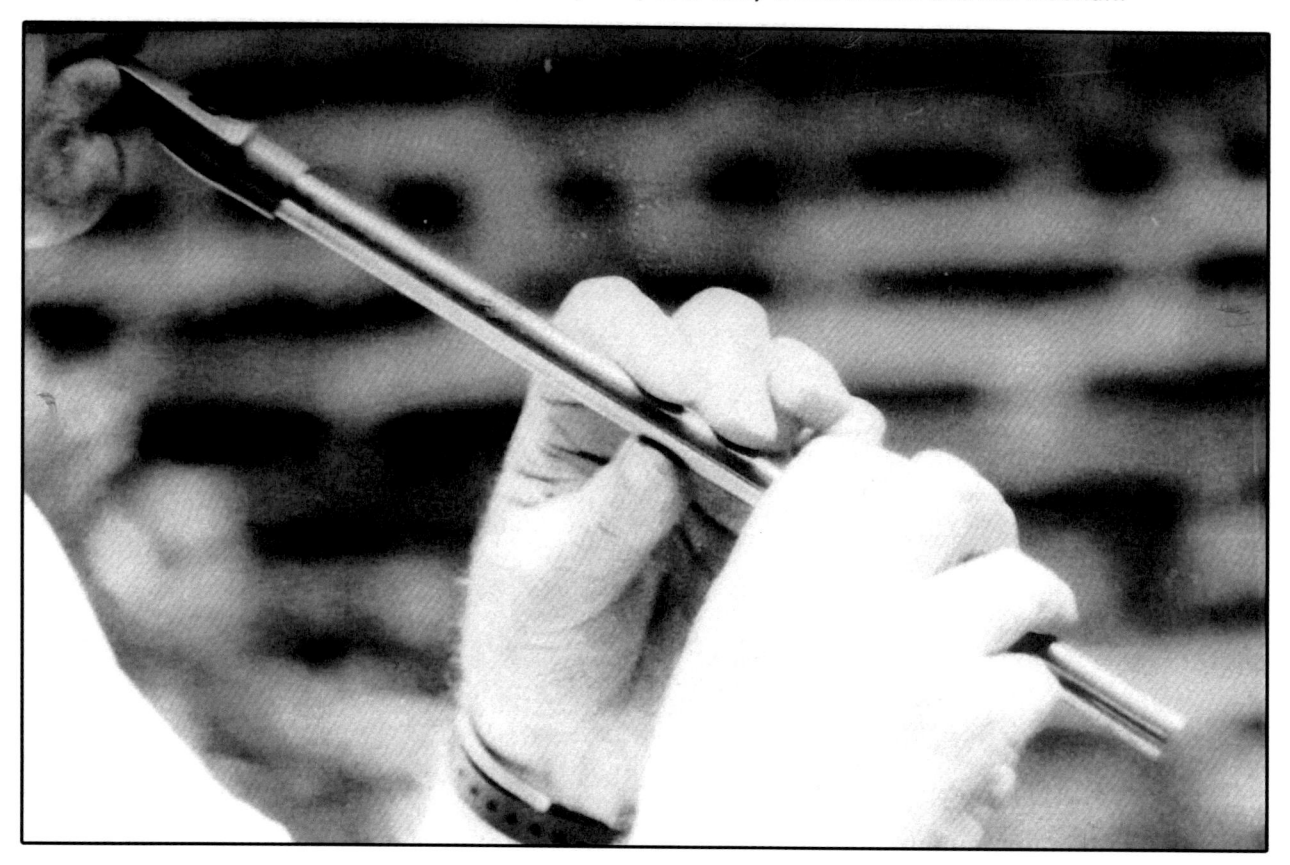

"Perfect posture"

With his cousin, Kitty d'Entemont, Saugus, Ma

Family reunion: Tom Clair, Katherine "Kitty" d"Entemont, Mary (Tom's wife), and thier daughter, Cathleen Clair. Saugus, Ma

With Dr. Richard Olsen, Ulster County Community College, Stone Ridge, NY

The new house up on the high road part of the land, built by Pakie, Gussie and Micho around 1960 for their mother; that she might have more comfort, and that it might increase the chances of her hope coming true, for Micho to marry and bring a bride home to a proper house.

In Ennistymon -- Co. Clare, 1984.

Micho in America -- Cottekill, NY, 1991.

With his mother's old one-row melodeon – Doonagore kitchen, 1989. (apologies for the poor focus but a rare instance I thought should be included).

Enchantment at O'Connor's Pub

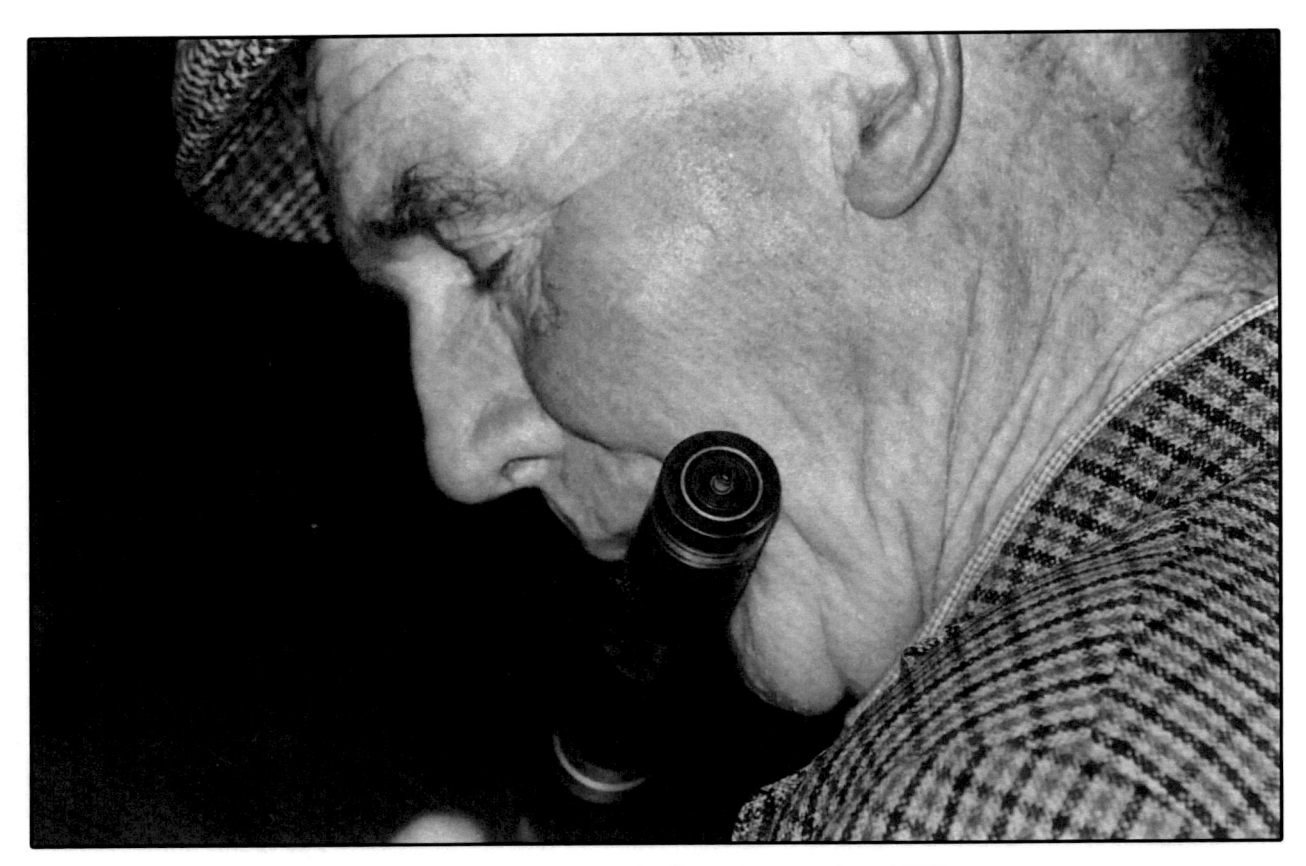

Gussie Russell – photo by D.C. Winter: circa 1985.

O'Connor's – 1980's

Paddy Shannon's house and birthplace – the last Fisher St. thatched cottage to be lived in, circa 1984.

Paddy Shannon, the Fisher Street Shanachie: the last best example of the native tongue; and the keeper of an enormous amount of local oral history and genealogy -- in the kitchen of his cottage in the lane, 1984.

MICHO RUSSELL, Legendary Tin Whistler from Doolin, Co. Clare

Photo: Dennis C. Winter

This photo (taken in McHugh's Pub, Liscannor, 1985), like Micho, has travelled the world. Bill Ochs had it made into Micho's 8x10 Glossy for gig promotions on the 1991 American tour, and it appeared in many published obituaries. It was first used for the cover of *The Piper's Chair No, 2* (c. D.C. Winter, 1986).

Micho and Bill Ochs: crossing Broome St. -- lower Manhattan (SoHo), NYC, summer, 1992.

Micho in America: with Ford Van, Louisville Ladder, 1972 Buick, Malcom X baseball cap, and flag t-shirt.

At Global Village Productions -- rehearsing on the patio for the video taping of *The Whistling Ambassador* ; this image also used as a post card – NYC, 1992.

Micho and Jimmy Noonan – a laugh over the fine points. Boston, 1991.

Gerry Dunleavy (Brud Petty's nephew) and Micho: "backstage," Saugus, Ma. 1991.

Gus and Doll's posed post card, celebrating the Pub's new façade, circa mid-1990s.

Gus O'Connor – always dressed for the work of Publican -- circa 1987.

Great friends: Michael Coady, Doll O'Connor, Séamus McGrath, in the lane, off Fisher St. – weekend of Gus Russell's funeral.

The Russell Brother's Community Center – Doolin.

"Where have all the brothers gone . . .

long time passing . . .?"

Farewell to Cottekill – leaving for Ireland and home, 1991.

Birthplace of the Russell Brothers -- Luogh, photo circa 2003.

The funeral -- Doolin cemetery, 1994.

Appendix 3.   Selected passages from my speech given at the Second Micho Russell Memorial Weekend, given in Doolin Church, by Dennis C. Winter, 1 Mar. 1996

"Rambles with Micho in America"

Good evening Ladies and Gentlemen, attending Clergy, fellow scholars and folklorists; and to a houseful of musicians, artists, educators, and to so many dear and beautiful friends of Micho Russell.

I am honored to be taking part in this memorial celebration, and I commend and congratulate this community and especially the memorial committee for taking on the work of preserving the spirit and memory of a man I feel truly honored to have know at all: a gifted musician whose contribution to life and art will always be inseparably linked to the history of this village.

The pre-eminent American folklorist, Alan Lomax, asserts that: "Music and culture are interconnected, in fact, that music is a communication about, [and] a mirror of culture." [1] I see Micho Russell as a natural and dedicated practitioner of that communication; and I think we could well agree that he bridged a kind of cultural timeline, so to speak, that reached back to an older form of expression and to distant, earlier Irish ways.

I related to Micho initially and primarily as one of his music students, which in turn led to writing and photography projects about him. My first essay, published in 1984, was titled: "The Whistling Ambassador," as that was how he struck me at the time, a kind of musical emissary of folk culture. It was a type of "pet-name" title which I doubt he was ever too comfortable with or all that pleased with, but I guess it just came with the job. Later on in 1990, I completed and published a small monograph, a biographical sketch called: *Doolin's Micho Russell: a Portrait*, but to tell the truth, though, I have always been just as comfortable being introduced as Mr. Russell's chauffer as I ever was as his biographer.

My friendship with Micho eventually grew to include becoming road-buddies, tour and gig mates, and for me, a kinship to him as a paternal or uncle-like figure from my own mythic and ancestral past. I am forever grateful that my sons were able to experience having Micho in our home as if some long lost uncle had come from Ireland and had come to visit them in America; one with a timber flute and a tin whistle and with songs and stories and a huge loving heart. Let us never forget Micho's tender patience and respect, and his unflinching willingness to teach and perform for children.

Many folks like me, who have met and spent time with Micho, often mysteriously relate that meeting as somehow life changing. His unique personality and presence, coupled with his Pan-like, authentic and charming music, affected deep emotional resonance in many people, often drawing tender tears. And in America, I'd say that effect was greatly enhanced due to the complete rarity of such an individual personage as this one-of-a-kind, the one-and-only, Micho Russell.

Micho's untiring search for understanding of the world through folksong and lore, constantly making his connections with history and human feelings, was the type of disciplined focus that signifies the major artist, be it folk, or fine-arts, they make and leave a major, indelible mark. Micho's amazing capacity for melodic memory and his impeccable timing and professionalism as a performer, entertainer, recitalist, and true showman, combined with his endearing manner and sense of good humor gives us the full effect of how I will always remember him: a world-class "musicianer," to use his term; and as a true storyteller, a real one, the kind who live the story again as they tell it.

Lastly, I'd like to say that our hearts were touched in America by this truly unique, gentle and musical man, who consciously and graciously represented his Irish heritage and culture in a genuine manner which, I assure you, you can all be deservedly proud of.

And in closing, I would only like to echo and reinforce Michael Coady's plea from his reading at the funeral, when he advised and urged us not to forget that: "We must remember the living man." I hope my reminiscence here has helped in doing just that, for that is what this celebration of our special friend, one of the great men of Ireland, Micho Russell, is all about.

Again, my sincere thanks and best wishes to you all.

1. Lomax, Alan. The Land Where the Blues Began, (Dell, New York: 1993).

Coda:

A few selected passages from the **Mass Eulogy**, offered by the celebrant, **FR. John O'Donoghue**(R.I.P.), author of ***Anam Cara***. Doolin Church, February 22, 1994:

"A tune that Micho loved to play, the Lord have mercy on him, was 'The LimestoneRock.' And the limestone around this place is very ancient. Today if you came to the funeral either up from the south or down from the Galway direction, you will have seen that there is an ancient conversation taking place here between the ocean and the rock. It is a conversation that has gone on for millions of years before the first person ever set foot on the stone of the Burren. There is an eternity here and it's now being recognized all over the world.

For generations this eternity has been expressed and mined by the people who have lived here – simple people, very often very poor and had very little. But in what can be a cold and bleak landscape, they kept something very warm and very tender and very beautiful alive. When you look at the eternal shapes in the landscape, it's no wonder that this corner of County Clare is famous for its music. Because in some strange unknown way, the energy and the light and the eternity of this place comes out in the music . . .

Today from that perspective is a very lonesome and sad day in the history of this area and indeed in the musical history of Ireland. Because we are laying to rest one of the lovely Irish musicians, who in a gentle and unpretentious way brought this great heritage of music out into the air and to the openness. And who brought it all around the world.

It's a very sad day from another perspective in that Micho belonged to a generation and a type of country people that are slowly vanishing. The gestures, the walk, the accent, the poetry of the language is receding and disappearing more and more. And another thing is that Micho had an awful lot of folklore in his head – old stories, and songs, and legends which came from generations back and brought the spirit of this whole area from around here out to shape and to expression. . .

He was a lovely man and I've never heard anyone – and I'm from around here – say a bad word about Micho Russell. Because they never had any reason. Because he was a gentle person for a big man. It's a lovely thing in a man to see gentleness in a big man. . . It's lovely when you see a big man who has a gentle and kind heart. And Micho had that.

Another thing about Micho was that he was generous with his gift. Sometimes when people have gifts, they get very competitive and they get very aware of who they are and who might be taking the stuff from them and have a whole competitive attitude. The Lord have mercy on Micho, he wasn't a bit like that. He'd play a tune for anyone, he'd show a tune to anyone, and he'd sing a song for anyone with an open and welcoming heart. And wherever he played and sang, there was joy and lightness and relaxation . . ."